Essays on the Historicity of Capital

Alain Herscovici

Essays on the Historicity of Capital

palgrave
macmillan

Alain Herscovici
Universidade Federal do Espírito Santo
Vitória, Espírito Santo, Brazil

ISBN 978-3-030-14837-9 ISBN 978-3-030-14838-6 (eBook)
https://doi.org/10.1007/978-3-030-14838-6

Library of Congress Control Number: 2019932974

This Palgrave Macmillan imprint is published by the registered company Springer Nature Switzerland AG
The registered company address is: Gewerbestrasse 11, 6330 Cham, Switzerland

*Para Denise, sem a qual tudo que eu digo, eu escrevo e canto
não teria mais sentido*

*À Denise, sans laquelle tout ce que je dis, tout ce que j'écris et tout
ce que je chante n'aurait aucun sens.*

*To Denise, without whom everything I say, everything
I write and everything I sing would make no sense.*

To Helena and Tomas, forever

To the memory of my friend Dominique

Foreword

This book will help in the first place all those who have some knowledge in economics but wonder which are the clear delineating lines between orthodox neoclassical approaches and heterodox approaches. Many tend to simplify this apprehension which may be confusing when many authors in the personalization of their approach tend to borrow assumptions on both sides. Moreover, a clear assessment of the theoretical differences between the two schools can clearly help to master one's own approach, as the book shows that beyond the standard opposition between orthodoxy and heterodoxy lies a great diversity of assumptions, depending on the problem under view. Still by no means is the book defending the possibility of a synthesis. Clearly it stands as a defender of heterodox approaches as the only ones, clearly concerned by the evolutionary and historical nature of the development of the world that we can observe.

Part I of the book gives various complementary epistemological perspectives that clearly set the hard core of each paradigm and list the auxiliary assumptions that are sometimes differentiating the approaches and somehow blur the lines between orthodox and heterodox approaches—clearly, a useful project.

Part II of the book focuses more on an essential dividing treatment in both groups, namely the definition of capital. Clearly, this exercise is not straightforward; it constitutes the major challenge of any approach in economics. This centrality explains the title of the book, as it echoes various classics from Marx to Piketty masterpieces.

To begin with, the book in its first part (in Chapter 2) stresses the sharp distinction between orthodox and heterodox approaches tied to their relation to history. While orthodox approaches are rather static and do not integrate historical contexts and trends, heterodox approaches pay attention to historical contexts and trends. Thus, while one does not know how the economy converges toward a neo classical equilibrium, heterodox approaches taking into account the diversity of behaviors and historical trends are open to bifurcation and instability.

Chapter 3 extends the critics of the neoclassical model on the epistemological ground. Using Lakatos concept of Scientific Research Program SRP, the author stresses how Keynes' and Stiglitz's arguments help to refute on various points the consistency of the neoclassical SRP. A review of the Cambridge controversy on the measure of capital in Chapter 4 completes these critics.

Part II of the book is more devoted to the history of thought. Chapter 5 interestingly stresses how biased is the interpretation of Ricardo by Marshall, illustrating one of the confusions that occur in the history of economic thought. Such disclosure is precisely one of the major objective of the book. Chapter 6 focuses on the radicality of Keynes's postures in his critics of the marginalism, be it for the efficiency of capital or of labor. These critics clearly raise issues on the patterns of information prevailing in the ways markets operate. Chapter 7 concentrates on the instability that these patterns of information can induce. Speculative behaviors and cumulative mechanisms can develop, producing complex dynamics as shown in various works by Stiglitz. Chapter 8 addresses contemporary issues in analyzing in a critical way Piketty's approach in his highly successful book on capital. The critics are three fold: one has to do with a relative neglect of the historical contexts, the second follows from the Cambridge controversy and the third concerns the empirical investigations mixing various kinds of capital. The short conclusion of the book praises the Ricardian, Keynesian and Stiglitzian economics for their strong way to take into account the heterogeneity of capital and its historical contexts. Such economics can lead to complex and unstable dynamics. It invites societies to develop institutional forms that could stabilize the working of these modern interactive economies. In an age when information plays a crucial role in modern economies, the development of institutional frameworks that could tame erratic market forces remain a major objective. Alain Herscovici's book of challenging essays helps to open this debate. It shows the importance of history of thought and epistemology to address these contemporary issues.

Paris, France

Pascal Petit
Directeur de Recherche, Centre National de la Recherche Scientifique (CNRS)
Centre d'Économie de Paris Nord (CEPN)

Contents

List of Figures

List of Tables

1
Introduction

1. From a methodological and epistemological perspective, the criterion that allows differentiating the different theoretical matrices is the conception of the nature of capital, more than the value theory, or the absence of such theory.

These essays will define this criterion from the opposition between the universalist and the historicist thesis:

(i) The universalist thesis is one of the fundamental components of the neoclassical school[1]: the neoclassical macroeconomic causality is based on the assumption that allows designing production function in which capital is conceived and evaluated as a constant quantity. It is a *reification mechanism* that conceives the capital as a "natural" process which remains the same over time, i.e., the same in terms of social value. Such natural conception denies the historical and social characteristics of the concept of capital. In this respect, Veblen (1908, p. 111) affirms that capital goods "are capital in the

[1]Even if we observe such conception in Adam Smith theory (1980).

A. Herscovici, *Essays on the Historicity of Capital*,
https://doi.org/10.1007/978-3-030-14838-6_1

measure, not of their technological service ability, but in the measure of the income which they may yield to their owner".

(ii) On the other hand, the historicist thesis demonstrates that capital is not a thing but essentially a social relation; this means that its value must change over time. This also means that a constant value of an aggregate quantity of capital is equivalent to the perenniality of the different kinds of social relations, i.e., to the absence of History.

This debate is related to the substantial hypothesis (Dumont 1985; Orléan 2011): the acceptance or the refutation of such hypothesis defines this dichotomy. I will demonstrate why and how the (neo) Ricardian and the Keynesian[2] approaches incorporate these historical components. In a certain manner, it would be possible to incorporate Marx in such historicist approach, insofar as his critic of the Classical Political Economics is based on the historicity of the economic concepts[3]; but I preferred focusing the study on the Ricardian and the Keynesian matrix.

Such theoretical debate is fundamental in regard to the construction of instrumental tools to interpret data and empirical phenomena: production function to evaluate GDP, catching-up in regard to the Solow's model and the convergence thesis, and so on.

2. Capital heterogeneity is a constant problem in Economic Theory, as observed by Ricardo, Marshall and Keynes. On the other hand, Stiglitz's works highlight the economic implications of information asymmetries: *such asymmetries represent another modality of this heterogenization process.*

From the moment when capital is heterogeneous, we must choose a common unit to express these heterogeneous capitals and to aggregate them. The temporal comparison becomes particularly complex insofar as the aggregate value is not constant in the different periods. As I will demonstrate, if capital value is the result of historically determined

[2]As I will show it in Chapter 7, I will include Grossman and Stiglitz in the Keynesian matrix.

[3]In regard to the historicity of Marxian analysis, and to some ambiguities of Marx's position, see Herscovici (2002) and Orléan (2011).

social relations, the aggregation problem may be formulated in the following manner: insofar as such social relations move with time, the value of an aggregate quantity of capital also moves. This is a patent manifestation of Historicity.

At the micro and meso levels, I will study such aggregation process from Keynes and Stiglitz's results. In regard to the macroeconomic level, I will use Ricardo, Keynes and Sraffa's works.

3. Besides some appearances, I will justify the methodological convergences between neo-Ricardian and Keynesian, and Keynes and Stiglitz; such convergences are not based on the surplus approach nor on the scientific program that conceives the effective demand as short-run fluctuations, and the prices of production as a long-run equilibrium, *but on the common conception of capital based on its historical dimension.*

In the General Theory,[4] Keynes refutes Ricardo's position in regard to the money neutrality (GT, pp. 18 and 29). It is also true that the concept of production prices is not compatible with the post Keynesian approach:

(a) from a post-Keynesian approach, there is not a predetermined long-run equilibrium position (Carvalho 1983–1984) represented by production prices. As said before, such point highlights methodological incompatibilities. I will focus my analysis on the conception of the capital, in the manner Ricardo and Sraffa did.
(b) From the moment when the value of an aggregate quantity of capital is not constant over time, it is no longer possible to conceive a convergence toward an invariant position of long-term equilibrium, as Solow did (1956), for example. The final position is a shifting equilibrium, which includes path dependence, and not a stationary one anymore.
(c) Consequently, it is no longer possible to define Ricardo's method as "hypothetical deductive". On the contrary, as demonstrated by Sraffa (1960), this method is historical: the long-term equilibrium

[4]I will write GT for The General Theory of Employment, Interest and Money of Keynes, 2009 [1936].

value depends on the changes in distributive variables. The historical dimension is present.

(d) Finally, Keynes, as Ricardo did in his differential rent theory, updates the value of the whole stock of capital in every period of production.

In regard to the financial capital, Keynes and Stiglitz's approaches are complimentary: Keynes shows why such value is self-referential and based on information asymmetries. Grossman and Stiglitz (1976, 1980) design models based on such asymmetries.

4. Theses essays will be structured in the following manner: in Part I, I will define, from an epistemological perspective, the various dimensions of Historicity. In the second chapter, I will study the nature of the scientific laws, in regard to the universalist/historicist epistemological dichotomy. Then, I will demonstrate how this opposition expresses within the methodological determinism versus indeterminism debate. At this respect, I will study what conception of Time sustains each position, from entropy laws and from Prigogine's works.

In Chapter 3, I will define the Lakatosian epistemological perspective, and I will justify this choice in regard to the Historicity; I will use such methodological tools to make a rational reconstruction of the internal History of Economics. Then I will define, from a Lakatosian approach, the Neoclassical Scientific Research Program (SRP): I will emphasize its internal coherency problems, more specifically in regard to the use of marginalist approach and differential calculus applied to Economics and, within a larger perspective, I will demonstrate how and why the (neo) Ricardian, the Keynesian and the Stiglitzian schools allow refuting this neoclassical SRP.

In Chapter 4, I will justify the epistemological convergences between Ricardo, Keynes and Stiglitz. I will show how each author studies the capital heterogeneity, and its implications, in the micro, the meso and the macro levels.[5] I will try to define the nature and

[5]If the micro level is individual, and the macro level the aggregate one, i.e., all markets, the meso level is related to the aggregation at the level of one specific market.

the function of the labor value theory used by Ricardo and Keynes, and finally, I will dedicate a special attention to Keynes and Stiglitz's interpretations of the financial speculation; these authors refute the fundamental value concept used by the neoclassical economists: at the contrary, the value is self-referential, and determined by inter-individual relationships.

In Part II, I will apply such epistemological choices to study how the three authors (Ricardo, Keynes and Stiglitz) explain and incorporate in their theoretical frameworks the heterogeneity of capital. I will follow a chronological order: I will begin with Ricardo's theory of differential rent, in Chapter 5. Such theory highlights the problem related to the heterogeneity of factors of production, and its results are not limited to the land, but linked to all types of heterogeneous capital. I will demonstrate why the neoclassical interpretation of Marshall is erroneous and in which way Historicity is a fundamental component of the Ricardian (and the Sraffian) Economics.

In Chapter 6, I will focus my analysis on the Sraffaian premises present in Keynes's GT: after studying the investment function designed by Keynes, I will emphasize Keynes' modalities of aggregation of the different kinds of capital, and I will draw a parallel with Ricardo's method. At last, from a simple formalization, I will demonstrate why such approach allows explaining the structural instability of the whole system.

In Chapter 7, I will bring to light the manner Stiglitz conceives the intrinsic heterogeneity of goods and capitals, from the *Relational Economics*, i.e., from the inter-individual relationships. Then, I will design a model to explain the different phases of the financial cycle, showing the incompatibilities with the neoclassical analysis based on the existence of bonds fundamental value.

In the last chapter, I will examine how the universalist thesis interprets the data linked to capital, rent distribution, and its evolution in the long term. From Piketti's book (Capital in the Twenty-First Century), I will highlight the methodological incoherencies, the erroneous interpretation of authors like Ricardo, Marx, Keynes, Harrod and Sraffa, among others, and I will explain why, and to what extent, such epistemological flaws do not allow a coherent and satisfactory interpretation of data.

References

Carvalho, Fernando Cardim. 1983–1984. On the Concept of Time in Shacklean and Sraffian Economics. *Journal of Post Keynesian Economics* VI (2) (Winter 1983–84): 265–280. Cambridge.

Dumont, Louis. 1985. *Homos aequalis. Genèse et épanouissement de l'idéologie économique.* Paris: NRF, Editions Gallimard.

Grossman, S.J., and J.E. Stiglitz. 1976. Information and Competitive Price System. *The American Economic Review* 66 (2) (May): 246–253.

———. 1980. On the Impossibility of Informationally Efficient Markets. *The American Economic Review* 70 (3) (June): 393–408.

Herscovici, Alain. 2002. *Dinâmica Macroeconômica: uma interpretação a partir de Marx e de Keynes*. São Paulo: EDUC/EDUFES.

Keynes, John Maynard. 2009 [1936]. *The General Theory of Employment, Interest and Money*. New York: Classic Books America.

Orléan, André. 2011. *L'empire de la valeur. Refonder l'Économie.* Paris: Éditions du Seuil.

Smith, Adam. 1980. Inquérito sobre a natureza e as causas da riqueza das nações, Fundação Calouste Gulbenkian, Lisboa, Vol I [Original: An Inquiry into the Nature and causes of the wealth of Nations, Methuen and Co Ltd, London, 1950].

Solow, R.M. 1956. A Contribution to the Theory of Economic Growth. *Quarterly Journal of Economics* 70: 65–94.

Sraffa, P. 1960. *The Production of Commodities by Means of Commodities.* Bombay: Vora.

Veblen, Thorstein. 1908. On the Nature of Capital. *Quarterly Journal of Economics* 22 (4): 517–542.

Part I

The Epistemological Dimension of Historicity

2

Preliminary Considerations About the Historicity of the Capital

From a methodological and epistemological perspective, the debate on the nature of capital is fundamental, with respect to the definition of the object of Economic Science, to the aggregate causality relations and to the design of empiric tools (Felipe and McCombie 2005).

In Part I, I will define, from the opposition between the universalist and the historical thesis, the nature of scientific laws; I will highlight the limits of the substantial hypothesis in regard to Economics. In Part II, I will show to what extent this opposition is related to the debate determinism versus methodological indeterminism. I will develop my argument from the two laws of thermodynamics and Prigogine's works.

1 Scientific Laws and History

1.1 The Universalist Approach

Hempel's thesis (1942) is Popperian: History only can be explained from the combination between some initial conditions, historically determined, and a universal law. The example used by Popper is the following one (1992, pp. 62 and 63):

A. Herscovici, *Essays on the Historicity of Capital*,
https://doi.org/10.1007/978-3-030-14838-6_2

1. "When a wire is brought to bear a weight that exceeds the one which characterizes its breaking strength, it will break."
2. "Such weight is one kilo."
3. "The weight attached to this wire was two kilos."
4. "This wire will break."

The affirmation (1) is the expression of a universal law; (2) and (3) are the initial conditions, i.e., the causes, while (4) is the prediction, in the Popperian sense. The specific prediction relates to some event which will be verified; the causality principle is explained from the relation between some initial conditions and this universal law. Causes do not exist per se, but only in relation to a universal law (Popper 1992, p. 62). The scientific law is, by nature, a-historical, because *it does not depend on some specific initial conditions*. Such causality relation is purely logical: it is a sequential causality, in the sense defined by Hicks (1979).

This is the *methodological monism*: the nature of scientific laws is the same, regardless of the objects and the specificities of such objects. These results allow formulating deductive mechanisms and using a purely logical causality; for such purpose, the mathematical tool is useful. The maximization of microeconomic functions is characteristic of such formalist *démarche*. The concept of substantive rationality, for example, can be applied to all kinds of human activities, independently of the historical contingencies.

To be scientific, a law cannot not depend on some initial conditions, by nature historical (Popper 1992, p. 131); but if a scientific law may be applied to all the systems, it does not allow explaining a specific one, in its historical dimensions.

On the contrary, Dray's thesis is intrinsically historical (1957). History is explained from individual's rationality, objectives and motivations. From a Sartrian perspective, History is the result of individual project and macro-social determinisms.

It is not possible anymore to use a purely causal logic, i.e., a sequential logic: the causality is random (or probabilistic) (Aron 1989, pp. 169, 170). The same initial cause may produce different effects; it is a complex causality (Herscovici 2002, p. 36); Because of the historical specificities, we may explain ex-post some facts, but we cannot predict them. It is a possible, and not a certain effect.

If, on the one hand, a single cause may produce various effects, on the other hand, one specific effect may be the result of various causes (Aron, op. cit.): we can speak about multi-causality. In such approach, it not possible to identify all the causes and all the effects, the rationality is obligatory bounded, in the sense defined by Simon, and the formalist method is limited.

1.2 Determinism and Systems Nature

We can differentiate two kinds of determinism: *the physical one and the mathematical one.* The mathematical determinism aims at resolving a system of simultaneous equations, while the physical determinism consists in determining the position of some system in relation to its temporal evolutions (Dahan Dalmenico 1992, p. 400). What are the relations between the stable or unstable nature of the system and the kind of determinism to be applied?

These two kinds of determinism are related to different objects: the first one to an abstract object, the mathematical one; Mathematics is the only science whose object is itself. On the contrary, the physical determinism is related to a concrete object that belongs to the physical or the social world: as concrete object, some measurement instruments determine the position of the system. In all cases, the initial position of the system will be imperfectly determined, as the measurement instruments have a limited precision: *in the Physical universe, this means that we can determine an area and not a single point.* If such system is unstable, it is sensible to the initial conditions (Israël 1992, p. 258). So, any infinitesimal difference in the initial conditions will translate into large divergences in terms of temporal evolutions, and into the impossibility to elaborate trustworthy predictions (or expectations).

The traditional dichotomy between Exact Sciences and Social Sciences is no longer pertinent: both have to face the problem of the measurement of some concrete variables. *The dichotomy to be considered is between Mathematics and the other Sciences* and between stable and unstable systems. If the system is stable, it does not depend on initial conditions and it is possible to elaborate expectations (or prediction, in the terminology used by Popper); if the system is unstable, it is not possible. The kind of determinism depends on the nature of the system. Contrary to Popper's view, we cannot apply the same kind of determinism ignoring the nature of the system.

To what extent may such results be applied to Economic Science? The formalism in Economics corresponds to the utilization of mathematical determinism; it provides the elements related to a universal law. From such a perspective, disequilibrium is conceived as a logical impossibility expressed in mathematical terms.

In opposition, historicism consists in using the two types of determinism: the mathematical one allows clarifying some causal relationships, while the physical one allows defining the value of the variables, i.e., *to make "provisional" closure of the system* (Chick 2004, p. 10). The value determined in this manner is not constant but expresses some historical specificities. In Economics, Mathematics represents an auxiliary science: it does not allow to substitute Theory or to ignore the historical determinations.

We can observe that if formalism is systematically used by neoclassical economics, it is used too by various heterodox approaches. For example, from a Marxian perspective, the transformation problem (transformation from value to production prices) is expressed by a system of simultaneous equations (Bortkiewicz 1959; Winterniz 1948, for example). Such resolutions are purely formal; they determine the production price which would be reached by the market price if particularly restrictive hypotheses are verified (Steedman 1984; Herscovici 2002). In the same way that in the case of General Equilibrium (Morishima and Catephores 1980), this formal resolution implies in determining a notional equilibrium that, probably, will never be reached.

The solution offered by the historical approach is quite different: in the case of the transformation problem, for example, the values of the key variables (the coefficient of transformation from values to prices) are not determined by an algebraic solution, but in an exogenous way, by historical variables: the state of classes struggle, in regard to the Marxist analysis (Duménil 1980; Lipietz 1983), or simply the exogenous determination of the distributive variables in the neo-Ricardian solution.

It is possible to justify this exogenous determination from the institutional approach: wages, for example, are not determined by supply and demand on the labor market, but they are conceived as a social convention: their determination is essentially institutional (Hodgson 1998, p. 175).

Contrary to what some authors called the "Ricardian vice" (Blaug 1992, p. 98), the Ricardian analysis is intrinsically historical, and not only hypothetical-deductive: as I will show it in Chapter 5, scarcity is not a natural fact, but a social one. In the same way, the value of an aggregate quantity of capital depends on the value of distributive variables, which changes with time. In this respect, Ricardo affirms that the natural price of labor changes in space and in time (1821, p. 78). *The historical dimension appears in regard to the determination of the value of the variables that allow "closing" the system temporarily.*

The debate between the two Cambridges illustrates such problematic: from a neoclassical perspective, from Marshallian foundations, the capital may be evaluated as quantities and integrated in macroeconomic production functions. Capital value does not depend on historical specificities and, consequently, is conceived as a universal concept. The Ricardian and the Keynesian approaches allow formulating opposite results.

1.3 Substantial Hypothesis and Economics

1.3.1 Dumont and Orléan's Thesis

Dumont (1985) demonstrates that Economic Science, since Smith's inquiry, adopts implicitly the substantive hypothesis: from the labor commanded theory of value, value in exchange is the power of a commodity to purchase other goods—its price. The exchange value of a commodity A is equal to the quantity of labor that A can purchase, exchanging A by B; A exchange value is equal to the quantity of labor incorporated in B. So, *Smith's concept of exchange value is defined from two dimensions: the production and the exchange* (idem., p. 225): A exchange value is concretized in the exchange by the quantity of labor incorporated in the production of B.

Consequently, labor is the common substance of all commodities. In other words, it comes to an objective definition of exchange value (ibid., p. 128). Exchange value is a relationship between things and not between men, *and each commodity has an intrinsic value defined from the labor quantity* (labor *en général*): this definition allows ignoring the social and historical dimension of exchange.

From such result, Smith will universalize the exchange social mechanism, from the "ingenious" example of a hypothetical primitive society where all members have a natural propensity to exchange: Smith tries to prove that "(…) labor is the value substance (…), and that value is totally disconnected from its social context (…)" (ibid., p. 228). *Such approach denies the historical dimension of the different modes of production and universalizes the social an economic characteristics of capitalism.*

The subjective value theory, based on the concept of subjective utility, constitutes an alternative theory. Such theory, developed from the utilitarian philosophers (Mill, Jevons, and Menger), is based on the subjective individual preferences: preferences are constant, exogenous and subjective. It allows resolving Smith's paradox of water and diamond: the subjective utility of diamond may be higher than water utility.

When the conditions of pure and perfect competition are fulfilled, in aggregate level, the first theorem of welfare implies that the system reaches an optimal situation, in regard to the Pareto criterion. Such mechanism works from the moment that the following conditions are verified:

(a) Preferences express the individual subjective choices, such choices are determined in an individual way, without relationships with other agents (Orléan 2011, p. 58). This characteristic is incompatible with strategic behaviors, or with any form of interdependency between the economic agents; prices translate the necessity intensity.
(b) The homogeneity hypothesis is verified: price conveys all the information which allow evaluating, ex-ante, utility. Quality determines the price: a high price signalizes a high quality. There is no uncertainty relative to quality; as marginal utility is decreasing, consumers will obligatorily diversify their consumption basket to maximize their total utility.

We can note that the *substantial hypothesis* (Orléan 2011) is adopted by both Smithian and Neoclassical Economics[1]; in both cases, it denies the historical and social dimension of goods and capital value, and affirms, implicitly, the universality of such value.

---

[1]At this respect, Ricardo does not adopt such hypothesis. Marx's position is more ambiguous, as demonstrated by Orléan (2011), but Marx's criticism of classical economics is based on Historicity.

1.3.2 An Historical Approach: Braudel and Polanyi

Braudel distinguishes three levels: the material life, the market economy and the capitalist economy. The first one is related to the material reproduction of the society, mainly to self-consumption; the second one to the competitive exchange, the competitive markets, and the third one to the continuous flow, to the primacy of the circulation activities, to the asymmetric information and to its international dimension, i.e., the capitalist markets (Braudel 1985, p. 22).

Braudel's approach highlights the historical (in opposition to universal) dimension of capitalism and capital:

- In regard to the second level (the market economy linked to competitive exchange), he affirms that "between 1400 and 1800, an important part of the production (…) disappears in the self-consumption of the family or the village, and does not enter in the market exchange" (idem., p. 22).
- On the other hand, market economy is a necessary but not sufficient condition to implement a capitalist system (ibid., p. 44). Capitalism is defined by the generalization of the third level, and not only by the existence of markets.
- As noted by Braudel (1979, p. 270), from an historical and theoretical perspective, *it is not possible to assimilate wealth and capital.* The concept of capital corresponds to Turgot and Quesnay's *advances*: it may be defined by a productive investment, i.e., capital as a production factor (Quesnay, cited by Braudel 1979, p. 271). Capital is directly connected to exchange value, i.e., to a capitalist system as defined by Braudel, while wealth assumes different forms in relation to the economic specificities of each society. The assimilation between wealth and capital is not historically and theoretically justified, leads to analytical confusion and allows identifying material wealth and capital: Kuznets (cited by Braudel 1979, p. 287) affirms that "(…) it is possible to question whether there was a formation of fixed and durable capital before 1750 (…)."

As Braudel wrote, the other modes of production before capitalism were characterized by the primacy of the use value (Braudel 1985, p. 22), even when markets activities were developed. The social forms of wealth had no relationship with the exchange value: for example, self-consumption, in regard to the anthropological concept of extended family, social use value or gift economy, in the sense defined by Mauss (1923–1924).

Polanyi conclusions are similar: in other mode of production "(…) the economic system is a simple function of social organization." (1944, p. 79). The economic system is *embedded* in the social system, and the partial systems (cultural, political, religious and so on) are not regulated from the economic system, but regulate it.

2 Determinism and Methodological Indeterminism: The Epistemological Debate

2.1 Time, Historicity and Scientific Laws

In all sciences, both exact and social, determinism is challenged. The two thermodynamic laws, the study of complex systems, the concepts of entropy and of dissipative structures highlight the limits of determinism, and allow designing an alternative paradigm.

Universality of scientific laws is directly connected to reversibility and to a Newtonian and deterministic approach. Reversibility means that the evolutions of the system do not depend on specific initial conditions: Birkhoff's theorem explains why, in the scope of the ergodic theory, the temporal average of the observation of an event is equal to its spatial average, and does not depend on its initial conditions (Arnoux and Chemla 1992, p. 51). *The principle of equivalency of all the states of a system* "(…) is the only foundation to explain the reversibility of the mechanical phenomena of determinism." (Israël 1992, p. 272). Karl Popper's thesis (1988, 1992), in regard to universality of scientific laws, can only be conceived within the framework of such an approach (Herscovici 2002).

On the contrary, the concept of entropy discovered in the second half of the nineteenth century allows distinguishing reversible and irreversible processes: the former is characterized by constant entropy, the latter by increasing entropy (Prigogine 1996, p. 27).

We can discern two different conceptions of time: the logical time as reversible, and the historical time, as irreversible. Irreversibility may be defined by the fact that the system can never pass twice in the same state.[2]

Such systems are unstable and present a hyper-sensibility in regard to the initial conditions. From a mathematical point of view, a deterministic approach is characterized by the fact that the resolution of differential equations has a unique solution. The multiplicity of solutions, which is the general case, is incompatible with determinism (Israël, op. cit., p. 260).

The initial conditions in which the system is can only be determined approximately according to the intrinsic imperfections of the measuring instruments. As there is a hyper-sensitivity to the initial conditions, the predictability of this second form of determinism (the physical one) is limited to the study of stable systems. Stability is characterized by the fact that the system is not hypersensitive to the initial conditions.

The "physical" determination of the position of the system is performed from an experimental procedure that is translated by a measure, quantification, in relation to the definition of a "concrete" object. Economics is an Applied Social Science whose object of study is constituted by the socio-economic relations of a certain society, which can be, with certain approximations, quantified and measured.[3] Ultimately, this distinction, in relation to the initial conditions, allows us to put the problem connected with the nature and historicity of economic systems; it also allows us to question the possibility of establishing forecasts in the Popperian sense.

While the discussions about General Equilibrium relate to an eventual mathematical stability of the system, with the possibility of obtaining a unique solution, *for heterodoxy, the relevant problem is related to physical stability.*

---

[2]This is what Nicholas Georgescu-Roegen called *irrevocability* (1971, p. 197).

[3]At this respect, Gordon (2000), from econometric works, demonstrated the limits of such economic measurements.

2.2 Bifurcation, Hysteresis and Historicity

The nature of scientific laws depends directly on the stable, or unstable, nature of the system (Prigogine and Stenger 1984). Thus, it is not possible to construct universal laws, that is, laws that could be applied regardless of the nature of the studied system; the question of the historical nature of the economic system becomes fundamental as it regards the construction of the object of study of Economic Science and the nature of the laws to be discovered.

Within a deterministic approach, the systems are conceived as stable mechanical systems, *whose qualitative characteristics are known and self-preserving*, and whose evolutions occur in a reversible time. On the contrary, the nondeterministic approach conceives the social systems as self-reproducing, self-organizing and self-transcendent instances (Bartoli 1991, p. 452): self-reproducing and self-organizing because the system manages to maintain the coherence of its internal structures as well as the coherence/compatibility with the external environment; self-transcendent because they have the capacity to develop more complex structures over time, that is, to modify their qualitative characteristics.

The historicity of such systems is explained by the concept of bifurcation. This translates the degree of freedom of the system, i.e., its "governing power" (Israël, 266): the existence of bifurcations is incompatible with determinism principle (ibid.) and it introduces history again in the analysis, emphasizing the irreversibility of the time and the evolutions of the system. In this regard, Prigogine defines bifurcations as "(…) points with probabilistic behaviors" and states that "The universe around us must be conceived from the possible and not by any initial state from which it could be deduced" (op. cit., pp. 67 and 81).

On the other hand, if the system is unstable, small modifications in the initial conditions amplify the divergences of the trajectories in the course of time (idem., p. 135); *irreversible processes of non-equilibrium* (ibid., p. 12) appear, and the evolutions of the system become irreversible.

This approach corresponds exactly to the conception of history that is based on the concept of "understanding": in this perspective, there is probability and not determinism with respect to the evolutions of the system and to the occurrence of some events (Aron 1989, p. 170).

The irreversibility of time and economics implies in hysteresis and hereditary mechanisms. In Physics, for example, "(...) the behavior of a twisted wire is different from that which has not been twisted ..." (Israël, op. cit., p. 267). In other words, the present and future states depend on the past states of the system. The mathematical implications of this phenomenon allowed to amplify the works of Boltzmann and were studied by Vito Volterra and Émile Picard, in the early twentieth century (Fig. 1).

From 0 to $E\lambda_1$, the system is stable; besides $E\lambda_1$, the system becomes unstable and two stable solutions, b_1 and b_2, appear: the fluctuations determine which of the two solutions will be chosen.

The bifurcation points are represented by $E\lambda_1$, $E\lambda_2$ and $E'\lambda_2$. Before the bifurcations, there are areas of stability; the instability manifests itself at the points of bifurcation; beyond that, the system becomes stable again. This phenomenon observed in thermodynamics highlights the historicity of the evolutions and the existence of self-organizing dissipative structures: (a) due to the hypersensitivity to the initial conditions, it is impossible to predict the evolutions of the system, that is, the type of stability that will be "chosen" by the system; the current state is the result of this historical evolution (Prigogine, p. 80); (b) *far from the position of equilibrium*, the system is not unstable but reaches other zones of stability, which emphasizes the concept of dissipative structures.

A deterministic trend can be represented by an equation that presents the following form:

$$x_t = \alpha + \beta_t + u_t \tag{1}$$

It is a linear function as a function of time; α and β_t are constant coefficients and u_t is a random term that follows a stationary distribution.

A stochastic trend is represented by the following equation:

$$Y_t = \delta + Y_{t-1} + u_t \tag{2}$$

δ is a constant coefficient, and u_t a stationary random term.

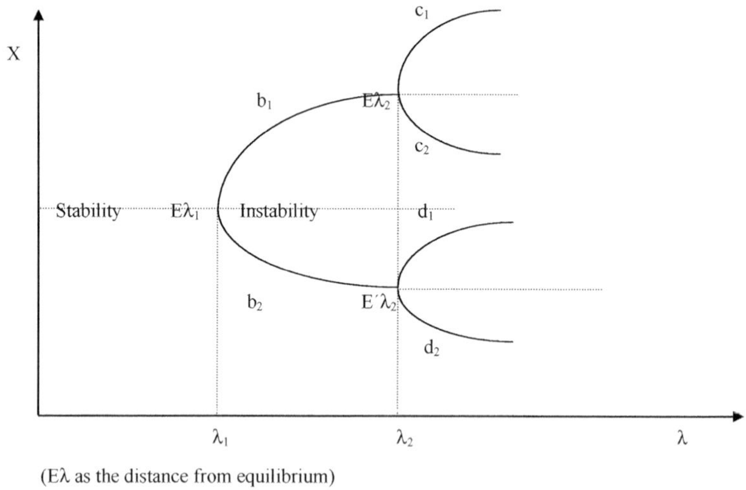

Fig. 1 Bifurcations, temporal evolutions and dissipative structures (From Prigogine)

While in the first equation, X_t varies linearly as a function of time, in the second, the value of *Y* in *t* depends on the value of *Y* in the previous period. The Cobweb theory is characteristic of this type of phenomenon and shows how the system can produce explosive fluctuations endogenously (Baumol and Benhaib 1989).

From this nondeterministic approach, it is no longer possible to differentiate cycle and trend (Vercelli 1999), i.e., fluctuations and growth: path dependence processes become fundamental because the value of the long-term trend does not remain constant during the adjustment process. From a methodological point of view, the existence of a gravitation process toward a given long-term position depends on the comparison between the rate of change of the long-term value and that of the short-term adjustment process (Harris 1988, p. 147): if the rate of change of the long-run value is lower than that of the short-run variables, the system adjusts over the position defined by this moving equilibrium; otherwise, nothing indicates that there is a convergence process. The different conceptions concerning the nature of the concept of production price illustrate this problem (Herscovici 2002).

On the other hand, the irreversibility is translated by the fact that the system cannot "go back" to the previous state: the temporal evolution destroyed this previous state. If, from infinitesimal variations, the system goes from f to f' and stabilizes at f', it can no longer return to f (Vercelli 1991).

Several statements made by Prigogine point out the following idea: near equilibrium position, laws are universal and processes are reversible; far from this position, laws become specific and processes irreversible (Prigogine, op. cit., pp. 12, 75, and 79). *The modalities of regulation of the system would be different far and near from the equilibrium position.*

Thus, there are two types of regulation, one reversible and the other irreversible: while the former corresponds to a neoclassical maximizing regulation, the latter is related to the reproduction of the system. This reproduction is totally dissociated from any process of micro or macroeconomic maximization, and can be translated by qualitative changes.

It is also possible to question the nature and role of the price system near and far from equilibrium: whereas, in the former case, prices variations allow a return to equilibrium, in the latter, the informational efficiency of the price system disappears (Kirman 1998, pp. 133 and 134). Consequently, the Marshallian market adjustment may work near of the equilibrium position; but far from such position i.e., beyond some critical value in terms of departure from equilibrium, the Marshallian mechanism does not work anymore, as well as the convergence mechanism. Far from equilibrium, another kind of regulation appears, different from the Marshallian one.

They are two types of approaches: one linked to the economy of equilibrium and the other to the economy of disequilibrium. Thus, neoclassical economics is an equilibrium Economics: the general Walrasian equilibrium is an *ex-ante* equilibrium, within a process centralized by the auctioneer's actuation (Duménil and Lévy 1987, p. 136). Transactions are effective only when the price advertised by the auctioneer is the one that allows matching supply and demand: these are "false exchanges" as the effective exchanges do not take place outside the equilibrium position. The theory of rational expectations starts from the same hypothesis because it assumes the hypothesis of continuous market clearing. Thus, *the mainstream eliminates from its field of research the problems related to the coordination and the performance of agents outside the equilibrium position.*

On the contrary, heterodox analysis starts from different principles: it is an economy of disequilibrium whose functioning is decentralized. The balance eventually achieved is the product of the agents' responses to an initial situation of imbalance. Consequently, the balance is carried out ex-post; the reactions of the agents, in relation to an initial position of imbalance, allow explaining the convergence toward the equilibrium (Duménil and Lévy 2000).

A dynamic approach allows emphasizing the internal contradictions, that is, the paradoxes of the pure equilibrium method (Vercelli 1991, p. 21):

(a) The Walrasian equilibrium is an *ex ante* balance; in this case, there is no way to explain why agents need to implement a process of *tâtonnement* to reach this position of equilibrium, if they know this position previously.
(b) Successive errors that progressively allow us to reach the equilibrium position do not produce a feedback effect on the equilibrium position (Arrow 1974, p. 4).
(c) The qualitative and quantitative nature of the information is the same near and far from equilibrium.
(d) Sim's paradox (1980) may be expressed in the following manner: the universe has to be ergodic for the expectations of the agents being realized and the rationality being substantive. Nevertheless, in this case, the imbalance caused by the unpredictable effects of monetary policy implies a form of bounded rationality and not a substantive one; substantive rationality is incompatible with the existence of monetary cycle, in the sense defined by Lucas (1975).

Finally, if, as Prigogine states, far from equilibrium, processes become irreversible, the nature of information changes equally: it is directly linked to institutional and cognitive processes and, as the universe ceases to be ergodic, it is not possible to identify *ex-ante* the possible states of the world: in relation to the problem of the General Equilibrium, we are in the presence of incomplete markets and the information no longer allows to reduce the uncertainty (Arrow 1986, p. 224). In this case, we move away from the ergodic world of the mainstream.

The relative permanence of certain institutions and conventions allows explaining the existence of periods of relative (and historical) stability during which social and economic regularities can be observed; these historical regularities corresponds to a relative ergodicity of the economic universe.

2.3 The Two Laws of Entropy

2.3.1 Definition and Main Results

The first law of thermodynamics "is essentially the affirmation of the principle of conservation of energy in thermodynamic systems" (Fermi 1996). In physical terms, this process corresponds to the transformation of heat into work: the coal that receives heat transforms this heat into mechanical work. Energy is "free" as it can be used to produce mechanical work; at the end of the process, it is bounded by the fact that it can no longer be used for this purpose (Georgescu-Roegen 1971, p. 5).

The conservative systems of classical mechanics verify the law of conservation of energy and are linked to the hypothesis of ergodicity (Sinaï 1992, p. 82): for these systems, within the ergodic theory, the temporal average converges to the spatial one and it is possible to predict the future from a calculation in terms of probabilities. In this case, it is possible to predict the evolutions of the system or, more precisely, the possible trajectories of such system; it is a stable system.

The second law of thermodynamics is translated by the degradation of the energy of the system: this corresponds to the transition from a structured system to a "disorganized" system (Passet 1979, p. 175). Entropy is increasing as the number of possible trajectories grows with the complexity of the system. When the free energy reserve decreases, the entropy of the system grows: in other words, the disorder grows because the free and structured materials become unstructured materials; a system with high entropy comes to substitute a system with low entropy.

Table 1 Entropy: a first approach (From Georgescu-Roegen 1971)

	Particles			
	U	X	Y	Z
Microstates number				
1	A	A	B	B
2	A	B	A	B
3	A	B	B	A
4	B	A	A	B
5	B	A	B	A
6	B	B	A	A

The following example may best illustrate this concept: let us suppose there are four particles, U, X, Y, and Z, and five possible states, A, B, C, D, and E. If we define the following macro-states "two particles in A and two in B", such macrostate corresponds to 6 possible microstates, as shown in Table 1 (Georgescu-Roegen 1971, p. 144). The entropy depends directly on the amount of microstates possible, that is, on the different combinations within the system.

In a first approximation, the entropy can be associated with the disorder and the absence of regulation. The different states of the system are qualified as microstates, while the macro state can be assimilated to general categories; the complexity of the macro-system depends on the amount of microstates (Prigogine 1996, p. 29). Boltzmann's statistical mechanics allows us to affirm the following principle: the disorder of a given system is proportional to the number of different states. The entropy is directly related to the number of possible states for a given macro state; the entropy depends directly on the amount of microstates possible, that is, on the different possible combinations within the system.

All the works related to thermodynamics, complexity and study of the nonlinear systems establish a relation between the existence of entropy and the irreversibility of the temporal evolutions of the system. When the entropy of a given system increases, the process is irreversible. The example concerning the mixing of hot water and cold water illustrates perfectly this process: (a) it is not possible from two liters of tepid water to reconstitute and separate again one liter of hot water and one liter of cold water. Such a process is irreversible; (b) the entropy, that is, the number of states of two liters of tepid water is much greater than the sum of the microstates of one liter of hot water and one liter of cold water; the entropy increased as a function of the mixture (Ruelle 1993, p. 149). In short, it is possible to affirm that, while reversible processes are characterized by constant entropy, irreversible processes are characterized by increasing entropy.

Thus, a system whose entropy increases would be characterized by increasing disorder. At this level two types of questions arise:

(i) What is the nature of this "de-structuring" and complexification processes that affect the system? Can it be systematically associated with a growing disorder, as stated in Classical Mechanics?
(ii) To what extent the effects linked to this process of complexification and disorder are the same for all types of system? Would it be possible to imagine different effects depending on the nature of the different types of systems studied?

It is possible to provide the following response elements: the concept of *dissipative structure* developed by Prigogine (1996) emphasizes the fact that entropy can produce other ordering modalities, that is, system regulation. The feedback effects and the self-organizing character of the system show that the disorder associated with the increase in entropy can produce other modes of regulation.

If the system is stable, small changes in the initial conditions cause weak effects and the system returns to equilibrium (idem., p. 35). If, on the other hand, the system is unstable, small modifications in the initial conditions can generate large effects (the hypersensitivity to the initial conditions), and the system moves away from the equilibrium position; far from this position, the evolutions are irreversible.

The second law of thermodynamics is interpreted as causing energy degradation and an increase in disorder; however, this would apply only in the case of isolated systems of classical mechanics (Herscovici 2002, p. 60); with respect to self-regulating systems, this increase in entropy can be translated into more complex modes of regulation (Dahan Dalmenico 1992, p. 395), as shown by the example of dissipative structures.

It is necessary to distinguish systems with null entropy by which future evolutions can be predicted, and those by which these future evolutions are not predictable (Arnoux and Chemla 1992, p. 56); this dichotomy is established according to the ergodic hypothesis. It is possible to establish the following typology:

(i) stable systems of classical mechanics have a predictable evolution, a null or constant entropy, and their evolutions do not depend on the initial conditions; convergence to equilibrium is independent of this initial position; this is the only basis for the reversibility of Laplacian processes and determinism. This universe is ergodic.
(ii) Unstable systems are non-linear and consist of at least three variables; although they are deterministic, their evolutions depend on the initial conditions; they are irreversible and cannot be predicted. These systems are characterized by an increasing entropy and the universe thus defined by non-ergodicity.

Finally, it is necessary to analyze the relationship that exists between the nature of scientific laws, the nature of the equilibrium, and the type of global regulation of the system. "While in the equilibrium position, or close to this position, the laws of nature are universal, far from equilibrium, they become specific and depend on the kind of irreversible processes" (Prigogine, op. cit.).

At the equilibrium position, the production of entropy is nil: there are no irreversible evolutions or fluctuations that could generate a deviation from the equilibrium position; far from this position, developments become irreversible. The system produces positive entropy; beyond some critical values, the processes become irreversible and the system moves away from the equilibrium position. The system changes *qualitatively* and produces other modes of regulation, qualitatively different from those that prevail in the equilibrium position. Far from balance, "disorder" can translate into a different order.

We can see the possible implications in regard to Economics:

- The convergence toward equilibrium is valid only within a zone determined by some critical values: out of such zone, the system becomes unstable, and the convergence mechanism does not work anymore. We can speak *in strange attractor*. For example, the Marshallian convergence toward equilibrium is not verified for the entire gap between market prices and the equilibrium price.
- *From such approach, the "crises" of the system is not explained by some exogenous shock, but by the fact that such critical values were reached.* In Economics, this means that fluctuations are not primarily due to some external shock, as argued by the Neoclassical Scientific Research Program, but by the limits of the self-regulation mechanisms produced by the system itself.

The open or semi-open models are historical models in which certain variables express the historical specificities of the studied period. The concepts of institution and convention perfectly illustrate this *démarche*: they are "extra-economic" variables that allow us to study concrete market, as they play a coordinating and stabilizing role. They change with time, which emphasizes the historicity of the analysis and the qualitative modifications of the system.

The relative permanence of certain institutions and conventions allows explaining the existence of periods of relative (and historical) stability during which social and economic regularities can be observed; to these historical regularities corresponds a relative ergodicity of the economic universe.

The methodological implications are as follows: the "plasticity" of institutions and conventions, from a methodological point of view, makes it possible to establish a parallel with biology: while the compatibility between institutions and the capital accumulation modalities explains zones of relative stability, changes in accumulation are translated by institutional changes in such a way that the new institutional arrangements thus produced are compatible with the needs of accumulation. The 'plasticity' of the institutions allows, at the same time, to maintain the internal coherences of the system and to create new coherences.

The analogies with evolutionary biology are as follows: increasing entropy, after a period of turbulence, creates new compatibilities and new modes of regulation; it is precisely the dissipative structures evoked earlier. In Economic Science, this method is compatible with the analyses of Marx, Keynes and Schumpeter: the structural instability emphasized by these authors can be expressed in terms of nonlinear dynamics and produces evolutions of this type (Vercelli 1985).

The historicity of this type of analysis is explained as follows: institutional changes are intrinsically irreversible as the process of change itself destroys the previous state (Georgescu-Roegen, op. cit., p. 197).

2.3.2 The Law of Say and the Stability of Equilibrium

Say's law can be conceived as the manifestation, in Economics, of the first law of thermodynamics: it corresponds to the conservation of energy and the stability of equilibrium.

(i) Say's Law implies a macroeconomic correspondence between the income and the volume of expenditure (Kregel 1980, p. 33): total distributed income equals total expenditure. In view of money neutrality (a) the theory of loanable funds ensures equality between investment and total saving; the part of the income that is not directly spent will be indirectly spent through the saving that finances the investment. The equivalence between the distributed income and the income spent, at the macroeconomic level, corresponds to the law of conservation of energy (b) in this case, the system reaches full employment (idem., p. 41) and allows maximizing collective welfare.

On the other hand, works related to deterministic chaos and dissipative structures allow us to formulate the following result: in the equilibrium position, property guarantees the regression of fluctuations (Prigogine, op. cit., p. 74). This corresponds to the first law of entropy and equilibrium stability: Say (1972) himself acknowledges that there may be sectorial imbalances but that these imbalances do not translate into an imbalance between global supply and demand.

From a simple formalization, it can be shown that in an economy with two sectors (production and consumption goods, in the sense defined by Marx), if global savings equals global investment, demand excess in one sector is offset by supply excess in the other sector, and global demand remains the same as the overall supply (Herscovici 2002, p. 264 et seq.). The results of this model can be expressed by the following equation:

O1–D1–(O2–D2) = Sg–Ig, Oi and Di as sectorial offers and demands, Sg and Ig as global saving and investment. *The local unbalances do not translate into global unbalance, and they are temporary.*

Thus, Say's law and the stability of the equilibrium attached to it correspond to conservative systems in which the production of entropy is zero; the construction of the object of study and the main results of neoclassical economics are directly linked to these epistemological references. On the contrary, structural instability is linked to the second law of entropy and methodological indeterminism.

2.3.3 The Ricardian/Keynesian Approach and the Instability of Equilibrium

2.3.3.1 The equilibrium has to be conceived as mediation used to be able to "approximate" reality: it is a valid temporal closure only at a certain point of time (Chick and Dow 2001, p. 713). It ceases to be explanatory when, over time, the value of certain exogenous variables is modified. It is from this conception that I will interpret the use and the meaning of equilibrium in the economics of Ricardo, and Keynes. I will demonstrate why such equilibrium is intrinsically unstable.

In classical economics, and more specifically in Ricardian Economics, the market prices convergences to production prices (or natural prices) and is based on the following assumptions: (a) competition between capital has already allowed the equalization of sectorial profit rates; (b) during this adjustment process, there is no technical progress or changes in the distribution of income. This raises several questions:

(i) Is competition a stabilizing process capable of implementing the trend toward equalization of sectorial profit rates? Does the market price system provide the appropriate signal to effect capital transfers in such a way that sectorial profit rates tend to be the same (Steedman 1984)?
(ii) What is the explanatory value of a dynamic process in which technical progress and changes in income distribution are exogenous and constant?
(iii) What are the implications of the existence of path dependence?

These modalities of closure of the system are made in such a way that the existence of this gravitation process depends on highly restrictive conditions; by the fact that there is no path dependence, they use a reversible, a-historical time, which allows questioning the theoretical status of production prices and the thesis that sees them in the long-term position, that is, the equilibrium price for the what market prices converge.

The absence of path dependence can be explained in the following way (Kaldor 1934, p. 124): (a) or the price system is established instantaneously, at each point of time, and each value of the exogenous variables corresponds to a certain value of the price of production. In this case, there is nothing to indicate that there is a systematic convergence process; (b) or changes in market prices do not change the value of the equilibrium position, which is unlikely in view of the interdependence of the markets.

In short, it is possible to affirm that the implicit hypotheses strongly limit the conditions for the existence of a convergence process. On the other hand, this use of the concept of the price of production allows conceiving these prices as supply prices: Marx, for example, supposes that in each sector demand is equal to supply, which is equivalent to the hypothesis of continuous market clearing (1976, Livre III, p. 167). Thus, there is an incompatibility between this kind of use of the concept of equilibrium and the historical method linked to the principle of indeterminism (Setterfield 1998, p. 528).

2.3.3.2 The same kind of observations can be made with respect to the concept of equilibrium used in the General Theory: the equilibrium represented by Effective Demand represents only the state of the system at a point in time. In the seminal text of Kregel (1976), three types of equilibriums are considered: the static, the stationary and the shifting equilibrium; in the first two cases, the long-term expectations are constant, they are determined exogenously, and they are not influenced by the changes in short-term expectations. The stability of the effective demand point is explained by the fact that short-term expectations do not influence long-term expectations and are exogenously determined.

According to Sheila Dow (1985, pp. 125–127), there are three temporalities in the General Theory: logical time, historical time, and "expectational" time. Whereas logical time is related to the static and stationary equilibrium, historical and "expectational" time is associated with the shifting equilibrium.

It is also interesting to note that the fact of exogenizing long-term expectations is tantamount to considering the shock, that is, the cause of economic fluctuations, as exogenous. This is incompatible with the approach developed here: as the analyses in terms of entropy and non-linearity point out, fluctuations are produced endogenously by the "normal" functioning of the system. In fact, in the economic analysis, an exogenous shock is related to the stability of the system; in this case, fluctuations are caused by an external cause: a monetary shock, with respect to the theory of rational expectations, a shock of demand in the New Keynesian analyses, a productivity shock in the analyses in terms of real business cycles.

Harrod's model must be conceived as a macro-dynamic model designed from the static elements present in the General Theory. Harrod's instability is explained from the fact of the capital coefficient being, by hypothesis, constant[4]; it is the reason why Solow (1956) refutes such hypothesis and, consequently, concludes that the

[4]For a complete analysis of Harrod's model, see Herscovici (2006).

system converges automatically toward the steady state. But why does Harrod adopt the hypothesis of a constant capital coefficient, and why does he consider that the interest rate is also constant?

On the one hand, the long-run equilibrium conditions are expressed in the following relation:

$$s/c = G_n$$

(s as marginal propensity to save, c as the coefficient of capital and G_n as the growth rate of active population and the effects of technological progress; G_n is an exogenous variable).

On the other hand, Harrod was aware of the impossibility to consider the valuc of an aggregate quantity of capital as constant and independent of the change in the value of distributive variables. He refuted the monotonic relation between the interest rate r and the ratio capital/labor, and he considers implicitly that the variations of the interest rate cannot verify the equilibrium relation for *all interest rate values*; it is the reason why he considers that r and C are constant.

Contrarily to various affirmations, such hypothesis is not justified from a technological rigidity,[5] but from the Cambridge controversy; for the same reason, in his 1956 model, Solow considers an Economy which produces a single good.

2.3.3.3 As I will demonstrate in Chapter 7, from Grossman and Stiglitz' works, in regard to the speculative cycle, that market equilibrium is intrinsically unstable; asymmetric information, divergent expectations and changes in the intensity of such asymmetries are incompatible with the stability of the equilibrium.

In summary, equilibrium stability is incompatible with the Ricardian/Keynesian approach.[6] Fluctuations are conceived as endogenous, and the absence of convergence toward a "notional" equilibrium implies in the structural instability of the system, in the way Vercelli defines this concept (1985).

---

[5]As Piketty argues (2014, p. 165).

[6]See, at this respect, the different models of instability designed by Goodwin (1992).

References

Arnoux, Pierre, et Karine Chemla. 1992. Systèmes dynamiques et théorie ergodique. In *Chaos et déterminisme,* Sous la direction de A. Dahan Dalmedico, J. L. Chabert, and K. Chemla. Paris: Edition Du Seuil.

Aron, R. 1989. *Leçons surL'Histoire.Cours du Collège de France.* Paris: Éditions du Fallois.

Arrow, Kenneth J. 1974. Limited Knowledge and Economic Analysis. *American Economic Review,* American Economic Association 64 (1) (March): 1–10.

———. 1986. Rationality of Self and Others in an Economic System. *The Journal of Business* 59 (4): 385–399.

Bartoli, Henri. 1991. *L'Economie Multidimensionnelle.* Paris: Economica.

Baumol, W.J., and J. Benhabib. 1989. Chaos: Significance, Mechanism, and Economic Applications. *The Journal of Economic Perspectives* 3 (1) (Winter 1989): 77–105.

Blaug, Mark. 1992. *The Methodology of Economics or How Economists Explain,* 2nd ed. Cambridge: Cambridge University Press.

Bortkiewicz, Ladislauss. 1959. Essai de rectification de la construction théorique fondamentale de Marx dans le troisième livre du Capital. *Cahiers de l'ISEA.* Paris.

Braudel, Fernand. 1979. *Civilisation matérielle, économie et capitalisme XVe-XVIIIème siècle. 2. Les jeux de l'échange.* Paris: Armand Colin.

———. 1985. *La dynamique du capitalisme.* Paris: Champs Flammarion.

Chick, Victoria. 2004. On Open Systems. *Brazilian Journal of Political Economy* 24 (1), janeiro-março, São Paulo, 3–16.

Chick, V., and S. Dow. 2001. Formalism, Logic and Reality: A Keynesian Analysis. *Cambridge Journal of Economics* 25: 705–721.

Dahan Dalmenico, A. 1992. Le déterminisme de Pierre Simon Laplace et le déterminisme aujourd'hui. In *Chaos et Déterminisme,* ed. A. Dahan Dalmenico, J.L. Chabert, and K. Chemla, 371–406. Paris: Editions du Seuil.

Dow Sheila, C. 1985. *Macroeconomic Thought. A Methodological Approach.* Oxford: Basil Blackwell.

Dray, W. 1957. *Laws and Explanations in History.* Oxford: Oxford University Press.

Duménil, Gérard. 1980. *De la valeur aux prix de production.* Paris: Economica.

Duménil, G., and D. Lévy. 1987. The Dynamics of Competition: A Restoration of the Classical Analysis. *Cambridge Journal of Economics* 11: 133–164.
———. 2000. *Déséquilibre et stabilité: proportions et dimension*, non published.
Dumont, Louis. 1985. *Homos aequalis. Genèse et épanouissement de l'idéologie économique*. Paris: NRF, Editions Gallimard.
Felipe Jesus, McCombie, J.S.L. 2005. How Sound are the Foundations of the Aggregate Production Function? *Eastern Economic Journal* 31(3) (Summer 2005): 467–488.
Fermi, Enrico. 1996. *Thermodynamics*. New York: Dover.
Georgescu-Roegen, Nicholas. 1971. *Enthropy Law and the Economic Process*. Cambridge, MA: Harvard University Press.
Goodwin, Richard M. 1992. *Chaotic Economic Dynamics*. Oxford: Clarendon Press.
Gordon, R. 2000. Does the New Economy Measure Up to the Great Innovations of the Past. *Journal of Economic Perspective* 4 (14): 49–74.
Harris, Donald J. 1978. *Capital Accumulation and Income Distribution*. Stanford, CA: Stanford University Press.
———. 1988. On the Classical Theory of Competition. *Cambridge Journal of Economics* 12 (1) (March): 139–167. https://doi.org/10.1093/oxfordjournals.cje.a035043
Hempel, C.G. 1942. The Function of General Laws in History. *The Journal of Philosophy* 39 (2) (January 15), 35–48.
Herscovici, Alain. 2002. *Dinâmica Macroeconômica: uma interpretação a partir de Marx e de Keynes*. São Paulo: EDUC/EDUFES.
———. 2006. O modelo de Harrod: natureza das expectativas de longo prazo, instabilidade e não linearidade. *Economia e Sociedade, Campinas* 15 (26): 29–55.
Hicks, J.R. 1979. *Causality in Economics*. New York: Basic Books.
Hodgson, Geoffrey M. 1998. The Approach of Institutional Economics. *Journal of Economic Literature* 36 (1): 166–192.
Israël, Giorgio. 1992. L'histoire du déterminisme et ses rencontres avec les mathématiques. In *Chaos et Déterminisme*, ed. A. Dahan Dalmenico, J.L. Chabert, and K. Chemla, 249–273. Paris: Editions du Seuil.
Kaldor, Nicholas. 1934. Alternative Theories of Distribution. *The Review of Economic Studies* 23 (2) (1955–1956): 83–100.
Kirman, Alan. 1998. Information et prix. In *L'Economie de l'information*, sous la direction de Pascal Petit. Paris: La Découverte.

Kregel, J.A. 1976. Economic Methodology in the Face of Uncertainty: The Modelling Methods of Keynes and the Post-Keynesians. *The Economic Journal* 86 (junho): 209–225.
———. 1980. Markets and Institutions as Features of a Capitalistic Production System. *Journal of Post-Keynesian Economics* III (1) (Fall): 32–48.
Lipietz, Alain. 1983. *Le monde enchanté. De la valeur à l'emvol inflationniste*. Paris: La Découverte/Maspéro.
Lucas, Robert E. 1975. Equilibrium Model of the Business Cycle. *Journal of Political Economy* 83 (6) (December): 1113–1144.
Marx, Karl. 1976. *Le Capital, Critique de l'économie politique*, Paris: Editions Sociales, Livre III.
Mauss, Marcel. 1923–1924. Essai sur le don. In *l'année sociologique*, tome I, Paris.
Morishima, Michio, and George Catephores. 1980 [1978]. *Valeur, explotation et croissance*. Paris: Économica.
Orléan, André. 2011. Orléan André. *L'empire de la valeur. Refonder l'Économie*. Paris: Éditions du Seuil.
Passet, René. 1979. *L'économique et le vivant*. Paris: Petite Bilbiothèque Payot.
Piketty, Thomas. 2014. *Capital in the Twenty First Century*. Cambridge, MA and London: The Belknap Press of Harvard University Press.
Polanyi, Karl. 1992 [1944]. *The Great Transformation, La Grande Transformation: The Political and Economic Origins of Our Time*. Boston: Beacon Press.
Popper, Karl. 1988. *Misère de l'historicisme*. Paris: Presses Pocket.
———. 1992 [1959]. *A lógica da pesquisa científica*. São Paulo: Editora Cultrix.
Prigogine, Ilya. 1996. *La fin des certitudes*. Paris: Editions Odile Jacob.
Prigogine, I., and I. Stengers. 1984. *Order Out of Chaos: Man's New Dialogue with Nature*. London: Heinemann.
Ricardo, David. 1821. *On the Principles of Political Economy and Taxation*, 3rd ed. Ontario: Batoche Book, 2001.
Ruelle, David. 1993. *Acaso e Caos*. São Paulo: Editora UNESP.
Say, Jean-Baptiste. 1972. *Traité d' Economie Politique*. Paris: Calman-Lévy.
Setterfield, M. 1998. History Versus Equilibrium: Nicholas Kaldor on Historical Time and Economic Theory. *Cambridge Journal of Economics* 22: 531–537.
Sims, Christopher A. 1980. Macroeconomics and Reality. *Econometrica* 48 (1) (January): 1–48, Published by: The Econometric Society.

Sinaï, Yakov G. 1992. L'aléatoire du non-aléatoire. In *Chaos et déterminisme*, Sous la direction de A. Dahan Dalmedico, J. L. Chabert, and K. Chemla, Paris: Edition Du Seuil.

Solow, R.M. 1956. A Contribution to the Theory of Economic Growth. *Quarterly Journal of Economics* 70: 65–94.

Steedman, Ian. 1984. Natural Prices, Different Profit Rates and the Classical Competitive Process. *Manchester School of Economic and Social Studies* 52 (2): 123–140.

Vercelli, Alessandro. 1985. Keynes, Schumpeter, Marx and the Structural Instability of Capitalism. In *L'hétérodoxie dans la pensée économique*, ed. G. Deleplace, P. Maurisson org., Cahiers d'Economie Politique, Anthropos, Paris.

———. 1991. *Methodological Foundations of Macroeconomics: Keynes After.* Cambridge and New York: Cambridge University Press.

———. 1999. *The Case for a Non Reductionist Macroeconomics: A Long Run Perspective.* Dipartimento de Economia Política, Universitá di Siena, não publicado.

Winternitz, J. 1948. Values and Prices: A Solution of the So-Called Transformation Problem. *Economic Journal* 58: 276–280.

3

Economic Epistemology

1 A Lakatosian Approach

1.1 Lakatos: Half Way Between Popper and Kuhn

For Lakatos, a rational reconstruction of the history of science can only be derived from internal history (1970, p. 92): "(…) external history is irrelevant for the understanding of science." Lakatos proposes to define criteria that enable one to consider these changes in selecting the broadest Scientific Research Program (SRP), which implies that science is an evolutionary and progressive process. Nevertheless, certain ambiguities arise with respect to this autonomy.

An SRP is progressive from the moment that it allows one to predict new facts. A progressive SRP in period t can become degenerative at $t+n$ as new facts on which it will be evaluated are changed, which enables one to relativize the concept of scientific progress and to ultimately question its autonomy. This progress is relative, as it is related to facts that change over time: "We thus have a demarcation rule between science and non-science, which is historical itself, involving the evolution

A. Herscovici, *Essays on the Historicity of Capital*,
https://doi.org/10.1007/978-3-030-14838-6_3

of ideas over time as one of its necessary elements" (Blaug 1976, p. 156). This historical relativity emphasizes differences between the natural and social sciences (Hutchison 2004, p. 183).

Other elements described by Lakatos himself limit the autonomy of science. Lakatos defines the hard core as "(...) 'irrefutable' by the methodological decision of its proponents" (1978, p. 50). Consequently, the criteria chosen to evaluate SRPs are not free of value judgments': "a rationality theory - or demarcation criterion - is to be rejected if it is inconsistent with an accepted basic value judgment of the scientific elite" (Lakatos 1970, p. 110).

External history at least partially determines the judgments of value that arc adopted by the scientific elite and the judgment criteria that are used to accept or reject different SRPs. If the scientific community is not homogeneous, several legitimate value judgments will be made. In this case, what criterion will be applied to accept or reject a particular SRP? Is it possible to speak about an *incommensurability* of paradigms in the Kuhnian sense?

Lakatos's position lies midway between Popper's and Kuhn's. Contrary to Popper, Lakatos's demarcation criterion has a historical dimension. That is, the conditions that enable one to define some SRP as progressive are not supra-historical. However, choices made among different rival programs are not solely determined from external variables, as stated by Kuhn. A "Mertonian" position is thus present, as there are "external social factors that promote or impede the development of scientific knowledge, factors that can be studied by the sociology of science, but the objective content of scientific theories exists independently of these social factors" (Hands 2004, p. 78).

From the perspective developed in these essays, the domination of the neoclassical SRP cannot be explained, nor justified, by the internal variables, i.e., by the internal history of Sciences, by its epistemological "superiority." Such supremacy is largely explained by sociological variables; *external variables become explanatory from the moment internal variables are no longer explanatory.*

We must observe that, contrarily to Kuhn's position (1991), Lakatos' epistemology allows explaining the coexistence of various paradigms; the dominant paradigm does not exclude the other paradigms, which correspond to the case of Economic Sciences. Lakatos argues that the empirical progress cannot be verified immediately (1978, p. 49): an SRP can be considered progressive or degenerative only after a long time, after the auxiliary hypotheses being modified several times.

1.2 The Centrality of the Scientific Research Program Concept

The SRP concept is the central tool of Lakatos's *démarche*. It consists of a hard core and a positive heuristic. The hard core constitutes the negative heuristic. It is composed of "(…) paths of research to avoid" (Lakatos 1978, p. 47), or that which is incompatible with the hard core components. This is irrefutable by definition and constitutes the fundamental basis of SRP (that is accepted by the scientific community). From this definition, auxiliary hypotheses protect the hard core.

The main function of positive heuristics is to protect the hard core against various anomalies that threaten it. This heuristic allows one to avoid the *modus tollens*, that is, *it maintains the hard core's integrity*. Its function is to define problems to be studied, predict new facts and thus integrate different anomalies (Lakatos 1970, p. 99). *While the hard core is fixed by nature*, flexible auxiliary hypotheses simultaneously protect the hard core while predicting new facts. The development and modification of auxiliary hypotheses must be compatible with the SRP's hard core, as this maintains the overall coherence of the research program, intensifying its theoretical development and its ability to predict new facts while preventing the Popperian falsificationism trap. "The positive heuristic of the program saves the scientist from becoming confused by the ocean of anomalies" (Lakatos 1978, p. 50).

One of the main purposes of Lakatosian epistemology is to construct a rational criterion for SRP selection and thus to develop a *rational reconstruction of the History of Science*. Using such a perspective, the *History of Economic Thought can only be conceived from its epistemological foundations*, i.e., on the basis of such a rational reconstruction. Drawing a parallel with History, I conceive History of Economic Thought as the long-term structuration of Economic Sciences, in the same manner as Braudel (1985) conceives Economic History.

The typology established by Lakatos states the following (1970, p. 99, 100 e 125): a program is *theoretically progressive* if it enables the prediction of new facts. It is *empirically progressive* when certain predictions come true (Lakatos 1978, p. 79). An SRP is *progressive* when its *theoretical growth* anticipates its *empirical growth*. Thus, the development of auxiliary hypotheses enables (a) the prediction and explanation of new facts, whereby hypotheses are compatible with the hard core, and (b) the verification of these predictions based on empirical observations. A program is *stagnant* when its theoretical growth occurs after its empirical growth, and thus when it can only provide ad hoc explanations.

An SRP is a structured and evolutionary system. It is structured in the sense that several models may develop from a common basis: the hard core (Hausman 2004, p. 202). It is evolutionary from the moment that rational reconstruction involves studying the succession of different SRPs based on two elements: (a) the progressive (or degenerative) character of an SRP is determined in a relative manner through a comparison of different rival SRPs, and (b) *implosion* occurs when a certain SRP develops elements that are incompatible with components of its hard core. In this case, regarding the positive heuristic, "(…) it cannot be given up without giving up the program itself" (Latsis 1976, p. 16).

Implosion marks the first sign of original SRP degeneracy. As the new SRP develops from failures of the former SRP, it is highly likely that this new SRP will be progressive and that the former will become degenerative. This phenomenon corresponds to the implosion mechanism. This *démarche* corresponds to the definition proposed by Lakatos: a new SRP can initially be grafted onto an older program:

> As the young grafted program strengthens, the peaceful co-existence comes to an end, the symbiosis becomes competitive and the champions of the new program try to replace the old program altogether. (Lakatos 1978, p. 57)

This implosion concept allows for the performance of *an endogenous analysis of the evolution of different SRPs* without requiring a hypothesis of scientific autonomy or, conversely, the primacy of variables external to the scientific field. Such a rational reconstruction constitutes a dynamic approach (Latsis 1976, pp. 15, 16) and enables one to explain the coexistence of several SRPs while combining internal and external History.

2 The Neoclassical Scientific Research Program

2.1 Some Preliminary Observations

The normative dimension associated with neoclassical economics can be explained and justified using the two welfare theorems that establish a causal relationship between General Equilibrium (GE) and Welfare.

> The two main theoretical results of the new welfare economics were the first and second fundamental theorems which linked the concept of a Pareto Optimal allocation to the Walrasian competitive equilibrium (GE). (Hands 2013, p. 4)

Social efficiency is directly related to Pareto's conception of social justice. Under PPC conditions, GE is automatically associated with a Pareto optimum based on the first welfare theorem, and as social efficiency is evaluated from this optimum; neoclassical construction acquires a *normative dimension*. Economic policies can only strive to preserve (or restore) PPC conditions so that a system automatically achieves this social optimum:

> The efficient market has again gained ground as the only objective scientific reference for solving social problems. If an economic policy fails to work, this is attributed to the fact that it was not designed in accordance with market principles. (Burgenmeier 1994, p. 351)

Different schools of thought that belong to neoclassical SRP share, from the same hard core, the GE and first welfare theorem. Using this theoretical framework, these schools of thought intend to describe reality while simultaneously providing normative instruments from developing different economic policies (Stiglitz 2003, p. 32; Blaug 1976, p. 176).

It is interesting to note that Friedman's epistemological proposal refutes this normative dimension. In his article "The Methodology of Positive Economics," he states that economics must be conceived as a positive science rather than a normative one (2009, p. 4). The validity of hypotheses (or theories) does not depend on their realism, but on their ability to produce predictions that manifest at an "acceptable" frequency in light of "*factual evidences*" (p. 9). *Under Lakatosian epistemology, these hypotheses (or theories) are directly related to the development of the protective belt, i.e., the definition of auxiliary hypotheses, and not of the hard core.*

In the existing literature, I have not found a strictly epistemological definition of neoclassical SRP. Colander describes "the death of neoclassical economics" and thus speaks of *orthodox economics, mainstream economics* and *modern economics*. The author argues the following: (a) authors such as Arrow, Akerlof, Stiglitz and Sen, who challenge the GE and its main results, belong to neoclassical economics, "*(…)* but each operates outside the "neoclassical framework" in portions of his work." (Colander 2000, p. 137) (b) The modern economy enables the explanation of uncertainty, multiple equilibrium, limited rationality, and information imperfections, and (c) neoclassical theory is dominant because there is not "(…) an alternative theory with a greater degree of falsifiability able to explain the facts explained by the previous theory and some additional new fact" (Lisboa 1988, p. 126).

The first argument is sociological, not epistemological. In this respect, Stiglitz clarifies that he proposes an alternative paradigm to the neoclassical paradigm (2003). The third argument uses Popperian and/or Lakatosian logics to highlight the superiority of mainstream economics. A reference to Lakatos is not valid until the hard core and auxiliary hypotheses of the SRP examined are not defined. The same type of observation can be made with respect to the second argument.

Those who can be defined as neoclassical are those who proclaim themselves as neoclassical without referring to clearly defined methodological principles. Such a "definition" is tautological and denies the possibility of conducting an epistemological analysis. *Because different SRP components have not been defined, it is impossible to define the limits of this SRP or to design a rational reconstruction of economic science based on its internal history.* This lack of epistemological definition extends the research field. However, what the SRP gains in breadth, it loses in methodological unity and normative power because the various developed models no longer share a common basis, i.e., the same hard core.

Although Stiglitz does not provide an explicit epistemological analysis, his studies include elements that emphasize the normative dimension of neoclassical SRP and that allow for the definition of its hard core and auxiliary hypotheses: the two welfare theorem(s) associate PPC conditions with Pareto efficiency (2003, p. 7) and the parable of Smith's invisible hand. As the PPC conditions are checked, the allocation of resources is Pareto optimal. *This forcefully implies that the subjective theory of value is adopted* from an ordinal conception. The GE is incompatible with the existence of uncertainty in the post-Keynesian sense (Arrow 1974a). Markets are complete (Stiglitz 1994, p. 29), which is equivalent to the absence of uncertainty. Consequently, the ergodic hypothesis is adopted.

A number of conditions must be verified for the first welfare theorem to function. These conditions constitute the protective belt. The concept of perfect information explains why the market is cleared. Similarly, there is no uncertainty regarding the quality of goods (the homogeneity hypothesis), and Property Rights (PR) are fully efficient and "free."

As I will show in Chapter 7, Grossman and Stiglitz (1976, 1980) demonstrate that the modification of these auxiliary hypotheses is incompatible with Pareto efficiency, i.e., with an element of the hard core. As Stiglitz states in several papers (notably Stiglitz 1994 and 2003), New Information Economics causes the implosion of the standard neoclassical program and simultaneously offers elements for designing an alternative research program.

2.2 The Neoclassical SRP

2.2.1 The Neoclassical SRP: The Hard Core

By definition, the hard core consists of irrefutable hypotheses. It is composed of the following elements:

The Subjective Utility Theory of Value

It is not possible to "prove" this hypothesis, as it composes part of the construction of the object of study and thus allows for the definition of problems to be studied. Factual evidencc, as defined by Friedman, will be conceived based on this theory of value. On the other hand, all neoclassical framework is based on an ordinal conception of such value theory.

The Ergodic Hypothesis

The ergodic hypothesis includes the main elements that allow for an understanding of how individual rationality may be exercised. Agents maximize their profit and utility functions by knowing quantities and prices in current and future markets.

The theory of rational expectations must be conceived as another representation of this maximizing rationality. Rather, rational agents elaborate expectations, subjective probabilities converge to the value of objective probabilities, and on average, their expectations are verified.

The GE is incompatible with the existence of strong uncertainty: "(….) uncertainties can tend to destroy markets, then we can conclude that the absence of some markets for future goods may cause others to fail" (Arrow 1974a, p. 9). In this case, no market clearing within the set of markets exists, and imbalances propagate to all markets.

The Marginal Method

The marginal calculus is used to maximize individual profit or utility functions; the marginal method (or infinitesimal calculus) can only be applied to economic mechanisms under the *ceteris paribus* condition (Marcuzzo and Rosselli 2011, p. 223; Martins 2013, p. 13). Sraffa refutes such condition, for the following reason: it is not possible to disentangle the contribution of an additional unit on the total amount of the factor of production; in other words, it is not possible to consider that all the other components of the stock of capital remain constant:

> 'pure' margins in which the marginal productivity depends not on the nature of each single dose of the factor, all being homogeneous, *but on the overall number used.* (Wicksteed 1914, pp. 18–20, emphases added)

This means that the variation in the marginal productivity (or in the marginal cost) is verified for all the amount of capital and consequently that the *ceteris paribus* condition cannot be verified. If an amount of capital is conceived as an independent variable, "serious difficulties arise in defining meaningful (strictly positive) marginal products when the quantities of the various capital goods are included among the independent variables of a production function" (Dvoskin and Saverio 2016, p. 1040).

The different update mechanisms I will highlight in these essays imply that is it not possible to adopt the *ceteris paribus* condition: the value of the whole amount of capital changes with time, in regards to an additional quantity of capital; on one hand, in the Ricardo's differential rent theory, for example, the productivity of all lands explored changes when we need to use a marginal quantity of land of worst quality (cf. Chapter 5). On the other hand, the updating mechanism itself, in Ricardo's framework, implies that, in some specific period, the value of *all the stock of capital* must be updated in regard to a "marginal" modification of the corn demand; beyond some critical value, the laws of succession (Bidard 2014, p. 3) are working which result in a modification of the long-term equilibrium. *The ceteris paribus condition allows conceiving the capital as a constant magnitude and justifying the perfect substitutability of the factors of production; in last instance, here are the direct consequences of the adoption of the substantial hypothesis.*

The Pareto Optimum

The Pareto optimum assumes an exogenously provided and determined income distribution, and these conditions correspond to the highest degree of social efficiency. This concept presents various limitations (Arrow 1974b; Sen 1982; Stiglitz 2003).

The GE construction only makes sense when using the positive heuristic definition: different elements of the positive heuristic (as methodological individualism and homogeneity hypothesis) facilitate the "operationalization" of the GE while associating it with a Pareto optimum, in the context of a normative approach examining the different market imperfections. This positive heuristic "defines problems, outlines the construction of a belt of auxiliary hypotheses, foresees anomalies and turns them victoriously into examples, all according to a preconceived plan" (Lakatos 1970, p. 99). Economic policies to be applied involve "flexibilizing" different markets to reach a PPC state.

Now, we must define auxiliary hypotheses that by definition are refutable. The positive heuristic ensures the overall consistency of SRP, that is, compatibility between the modification of these hypotheses and elements of the hard core.

2.2.2 The Auxiliary Hypotheses

The Macroeconomic Adjustment

From a macroeconomic perspective, the loanable funds theory allows the macroeconomic adjustment toward the full employment equilibrium (Herscovici 2006). In the same manner, the perfect substitutability of factors of production explains why, from well comported production functions, the system reaches the steady-state equilibrium (Bidard 2014, p. 11).

On the other hand, in Keynes' mechanisms, the effects of a variation of the interest rate on the capital are extensive and not intensive: a decrease of the interest rate will induce an increase of the investment, and not systematically an increase of the ratio capital/labor (Pasinetti 1997).

We must observe that such functions are designed from microeconomic foundations, and that such micro-foundations are based on the decreasing marginal productivity law and the law of constant returns of scale. As I will show in Chapter 5, such laws were refuted by Ricardo and Sraffa.

Methodological Individualism and Homogeneity

An individual preference is qualified as objective when it is exogenous and when it does not depend on the preferences of other agents (Orléan 2011, p. 58). Relationships between agents are substituted by the existence of the auctioneer (*crieur de prix,* in the terminology used by Walras), which enables decisions of supply and demand to be confronted and reconciled, thus ensuring a continuous market clearing.

Homogeneity, Prices, Quality and Equilibrium

According to Lancaster's analysis (Orléan 2011, pp. 61, 62), the characteristics of goods are the same for all consumers. *Quality is given*; each consumer will choose a basket of goods according to their subjective preferences. There is thus an objective means of determining utility: the characteristics, that is, the qualities of goods, are the same for all consumers. The subjective dimension derives from the fact that consumer choices differ: "(…) so that the personal element in consumer choice arises in the choice between collections of characteristics only, not in the allocation of characteristics to the goods" (Lancaster, cited in Orléan 2011, p. 62). *Hypothetically, there is no uncertainty surrounding the determination of quality.*

The price system provides all necessary information with respect to the quality of goods and services: *price directly depends on quality* (Stiglitz 1987, p. 2). According to Grossman and Stiglitz (1976, 1980) and Stiglitz (1987, 2011), the modification of such a hypothesis is incompatible with the Pareto Optimum.

Each price corresponds to a given quality. It is possible to speak of quality "objectification,"[1] and homogeneity is defined from this *univocal* relationship between price and quality:

$$p = \varphi(q) \tag{1}$$

where q is quality and p is price.

Self-Enforcement

Neoclassical SRP is based on the self-enforcement hypothesis: certain general and essential conditions are ensured and are completely efficient without involving any private or social cost (Bowles and Ginty 1993).

Transaction Costs (TC) related to market functionality and trade implementations are in principle null. According to Coase, this hypothesis corresponds, in the realm of physics, to the fact that the movement of bodies occurs without friction (1988).

In principle, a lack of high uncertainty means that contracts and markets are complete. Consequently, PR are fully efficient because producers control all appropriation modalities of their production. These approaches to PR are implemented at no cost. They enable the set of externalities to be internalized, and social utility coincides with individual utility.

The homogeneity hypothesis is an essential element of neoclassical SRP. It implies that the system of prices provides information related to quality at no cost. Conversely, when the economy is "relational," quality depends on the behaviors of agents who take part in transactions. By definition, contracts are incomplete (Williamson 2002), and TC are mandatorily positive. Rather, they involve monitoring the behavior of opportunistic agents and "controlling" behavioral uncertainty (Barzel 1997).

---

[1]It is the term used by Orléan (2011, pp. 96, 97).

2.2.3 Economic Sciences: An Analysis in Terms of Internal History

The neoclassical SRP is represented in Table 1. There are two manners of modifying the auxiliary hypotheses: the first one consists in modifying such hypotheses in such a way that these modifications are compatible with *all the components* of the hard core.

There are equally two ways to refute the neoclassical SRP:

a. The first one implies in modifying auxiliary hypotheses in such manner that some results become incompatible with some components of the hardcore; it is what Akerlof, Grossman and Stiglitz, Coase and Williamson did; it is what I called the implosion of the mainstream (Herscovici 2015).
b. Ricardo, Sraffa and Keynes refuted the neoclassical SRP in a different way: from premises which do not belong to the neoclassical SRP (or, more precisely, to the neoclassical hardcore), they designed critics directly related to the main mechanisms advanced by neoclassical SRP. From different hard core, they refute the method used by neoclassical economics, as well as its principal hypotheses and results.

Confronted with these threats, neoclassical authors develop immunization strategies to maintain the internal coherence of the neoclassical SRP; Weintraub states that the hard core of neoclassical SRP (which he describes as neo-Walrasian) is always under construction, i.e., is not fixed: "Consequently it must be the case that the hard core is not so fixed as a traditional Lakatosian appraisal may seem to suggest" (1985, p. 36). It is not possible to define the hard core and the positive heuristic, as the hard core is "fluctuating"; therefore, a particular component may belong either to the hard core or to the protective belt. Backhouse (2004, p. 178) adopts a similar position: "Lakatos's definition of a research program in terms of an invariant hard core is too narrow." I consider such position to be an *immunization strategy*. When an anomaly threatens the hard core, a modification of this hard core enables such a threat to be avoided.

Table 1 The neoclassical SRP

Hard core	Auxiliary hypotheses	Modifications of the auxiliary hypotheses	
		Flexibilization	Refutation
*Substantive Rationality	– Fixed individual preferences – Maximizing rationality		
*Marginal calculus	Ceteris paribus condition (Marshall)		Sraffa/Keynes
*Ergodicity	Contingent markets (Arrow)		Keynes
	Homogeneity postulate		Akerlof, Stiglitz
	→ Prices depend on quantities		
	→ Perfect information	Imperfect information (Stigler Salop, Friedman Lucas)	
	→ Law of single price		
*Subjective theory of value	– An ordinal conception – Decreasing marginal utility		
*Law of supply and demand	– Assessment independent of supply and demand		Stiglitz
	– Perfect price flexibility/ market adjustment	IS/LM Short term rigidities Menu costs (Mankiw)	Atypical supply and demand curves (Stiglitz)
	– Continuous market clearing	Menu costs (Mankiw)	Stiglitz Rationed market
	– Increasing marginal costs (decreasing marginal productivity)		Ricardo-Sraffa
	– Constant returns of scale		Ricardo-Sraffa
	– Self-enforcement		Stiglitz/Coase/ Williamson
	→ Null transaction costs		Coase
	→ Complete contracts		Williamson
	→ Property Rights system efficient		

(continued)

Table 1 (continued)

Hard core	Auxiliary hypotheses	Modifications of the auxiliary hypotheses	
		Flexibilization	Refutation
*General Equilibrium			
	Loanable funds theory		Sraffa-Keynes
Perfect substitutability of production factors $\Rightarrow$ Pareto optimum			Sraffa-Keynes

This type of choice purposefully confuses models with SRP. Rather, an SRP is related to long-term movements and internal dynamics that explain its evolution. An SRP represents the common matrix (the term used by Kuhn) from which different models are developed. An SRP enables one to develop various theories and models. In contrast, models are isolated elements that are related to "short term" and share the same common matrix. *Ultimately, based on an epistemological criterion, it is impossible to define a model as neoclassical without previously defining the original matrix that it comes from.*

3 The Refutation of the Neoclassical SRP

3.1 Neo-Ricardian and Keynesian: The Closure of the Aggregate Model

The problem related to the modalities *of closure of the system* is fundamental: such modalities allow differentiating the neoclassical SRP and the Ricardian and Keynesian ones. The former conceives the economic system as a *closed one*: all the relevant variables can be identified, the dichotomy between exogenous and endogenous variables is fixed and the way the exogenous variables affect the whole system may be forecasted (Chick 2004, p. 6). It is the reason why the closure of the system may be expressed by the mathematical resolution of a system composed by simultaneous equations.

The closure is logical and not historical; it is the method used to determinate prices and quantities from the GE, the transformation problem as well as the way the neoclassical SRP interprets and integrates the Keynesian framework (Dow and Chick 2001).

On the contrary, Ricardian and Keynesian SRP conceive the economic system as open. The closure of the system is provisional, and "The provisional character of the closure makes any equilibrium obtained under its assumption also provisional" (Chick 2004, p. 11). In other words, History resurfaces when some exogenous variables change; consequently, the own equilibrium changes. We can see the frontal opposition between a formal logic and an historical logic.

The neoclassical macroeconomic model is hierarchic and, dichotomous: in a first time, in the short run, in a situation of pure and perfect competition, equilibrium is determined on the labor market; then, from the quantity of labor exchanged, the equilibrium is realized on goods and services market, from a well comported production function. Such markets represent the real sphere, and because of the neutrality of money, the monetary variables cannot modify the real ones.

The macroeconomic adjustment is realized by the loanable funds theory: the "natural" interest rate is determined in such a way that the aggregate supply price is equal to aggregate demand, *for all levels of output* (GT, p. 24). This is the direct manifestation of Say's Law, and it implies that the system adjusts automatically until full employment is realized.

3.2 The Foundations of the Ricardian/Keynesian Refutation

The Ricardian and the Keynesian frameworks are characterized by other modalities of closure of the system, both historical.

In the Ricardian/Sraffaian Economics, Investment is not automatically equal to Saving *for all levels of product*: insofar as there is not a monotonic relation between interest rate and investment, the system does not achieve automatically the equilibrium position with full employment (Petri 1988). If, for example, Investment is greater than saving, the neoclassical adjustment works because the increase of the interest rate will imply in a decrease of investment; but according to the reswitching of techniques, such relation is not systematically verified.

In the same manner, in Chapter 14 of the GT, Keynes refutes the loanable funds theory. This refutation is a crucial moment of this "Keynesian revolution": from this moment, he refutes all the causality of the (neo) classical aggregate model.

Keynes refutes also the second postulates of the "Classical" Theory: the labor supply is not determined by the equality between the real wage and the labor disutility (GT, Chapter 2). As Keynes summarizes, the Classical Theory depends on the following assumptions (GT, p. 21): (a) The real wage is equal to the disutility of employment (b) There is not involuntary unemployment and (c) Supply creates its own demand.

From such methodological observations, we can deduce the commons components of the Ricardian and the Keynesian SRP, and its incompatibilities with the neoclassical one. We can argue that Keynes, in the same manner as Ricardo, refutes the existence of a labor market, as well as a capital market, in the neoclassical sense (Barrère 1985). In the same manner, in the Ricardian model, distributive variables are determined in an exogenous manner and change with time (Ricardo 1821).

The global macro-causalities are totally different: from the neoclassical perspective, goods and services markets equilibrium depends on the previous full employment equilibrium realized on the labor market, and the distributive variables are determined from the competitive labor market mechanisms. From the Ricardian and Keynesian perspective, we can observe different causalities:

- In Ricardo's framework, the goods and service markets depend on the exogenous, and historical determination of the distributive variables, and not on the labor market per se.
- In Keynes' General Theory, in a first time, in regard to capitalist's long-term expectations, the Effective Demand is determined. Then, such effective Demand corresponds to a determinate level of product and employment; the logical hierarchy is inverted: the employment level depends on the long-term expectations elaborated by the entrepreneurs on the goods and services market.

On the other hand, Keynes argues that the labor supply is not determined from the real wages, because real wages are not known when the labor contract is realized. Finally, in regard to the problem related to the value of some quantity of aggregate capital, Keynes will measure the increase of output by the increase in employment (GT, p. 35). In the GT framework, the level of employment depends on the effective demand: employment is a determined and not a determinant variable.

Such framework is incompatible with the neoclassical distribution theory: the remuneration of the factors of production is not determined by its respective contributions to the product (The Walrasian theory of the *services producteurs*), as Clark argued (1891 p. 313): "What a social class gets is, *under natural laws*, what it contributes to the general output of industry" (emphasis added). One more time, we can note that in such approach, economic laws are conceived as natural laws, which are related to the substantial hypothesis.

We must observe that such mechanism is directly connected to the existence of an invariant value of some quantities of capital and labor and that the distribution is determined by the "(…) relative 'factor endowments'" (Harris 1978, p. 219), i.e., by the quantities of factors multiplied by their respective unitary prices. One more time, we see that the neoclassical model, and its implications in terms of product and distribution, is based on aggregate factors evaluated in "physical" quantities.

In both Ricardo and Keynes, the distributive variables are determined in an exogenous way: in the GT, as I will demonstrate formally, the interest rate is conceived as an exogenous variable. In the Ricardian tradition, distributive variables are also exogenous. On a more concrete level, the exogenous characteristics of these variables may be explained by the presence of conventions and institutions in its historical dimensions.

We can conclude that, from the Ricardian/Keynesian perspective, the closure of the system is realized from a *historical logic*: the exogenous variables depend on some specific historical conditions: the level of development for Ricardo, the state of expectations for Keynes. On the contrary, neoclassical modalities of closure of the system use a *formal logic*, generally the mathematical resolution.

The different attempts to integrate the Ricardian/Keynesian model into the neoclassical framework fail because they do not maintain the same macro-causalities;

i. In Chapter 5, I will highlight the limits of Marshall's interpretation of Ricardo's differential rent theory, i.e., the limits of the neoclassical interpretation of Ricardo. Such interpretation occults the problem related to the heterogeneity of capital, to enable conceiving Ricardo as a precursor of the marginalist analysis.
ii. The explicative value of the Keynesian Economics is limited to the short run, and the path dependence is not considered: "(…) all economist theory, whatever model they prefer for the short-run analysis, accepts the quantity-theory model, completed by the Walrasian equations, as valid for long-run equilibrium" (Friedman 1974, p. 44).
The same hypotheses are used by some new Keynesian economists: Mankiw, for *example, justifies price rigidity, in the short run, by the existence of menu costs; so, short-run fluctuations are explained by an imperfect flexibility of prices. But such fluctuations disappear in the long run and do not modify the long-run equilibrium* (Mankiw 1985).
iii. Keynesian uncertainty, in the sense defined by Knight, disappears in the long run: "At long-run equilibrium position, all anticipations are realized, so the actual and anticipated magnitudes (…) are equal" (Friedman 1974, p. 48).
iv. In the same manner, the demand for money depends on the interest rate (Hicks 1937), and such interest rate is determined, endogenously, on the Investment/Saving market (GT, Chapter 14). Equilibrium on the investment/saving market is determined in such a way to realize automatically the equilibrium between aggregate demand and supply, and the full employment equilibrium.

The causality used in the GT is different: the interest rate is determined exogenously, by the uncertainty, and such value of the interest rate will determine investment, production and employment. Considering such mechanisms, the equilibrium that characterizes the point of effective demand does not correspond automatically to full employment. We can also affirm that, in the GT, in regard to the function of store of wealth of the money, the demand for money determines the level of the interest rate which allows realizing the equilibrium on the monetary market (GT, Chapter 13; Herscovici 2006).

3.3 Stiglitz and the Refutation of the Neoclassical Micro-Foundations

The neoclassical current of Information Economics includes the following assumptions (Stigler 1961): there is no uncertainty because consumers equate the cost of information with its marginal utility (p. 216), and *products are, by definition, homogenous* (p. 222). Although such studies are considered to be seminal, their explanatory limitations soon appeared. This can be concluded from the fact that the main principles of neoclassical economics were maintained: a lack of uncertainty and the homogeneity of goods and services. This allows fixed and objective individual preferences to be maintained, thus disregarding information asymmetries related to moral hazard and its implications with regards to the quality of goods services and capitals. When neoclassical SRP studies information imperfections, it cannot consider information asymmetries because these are incompatible with the Pareto optimum.

The epistemological rupture from which the implosion mechanism is developed initiates with the works of Salop and becomes effective in the works of Akerlof and Stiglitz. Then, the Information Economics, from the seminal results of Akerlof, Grossman and Stiglitz, constitutes an internal criticism, and is representative of the implosion of the neoclassical SRP.

Such criticism extends with some new institutional developments, and more particularly with Coase and Williamson's works.[2] From his criticism of Pigou, Coase (1960) refutes the individual subjective theory of value, and he proposes an alternative definition of the nature of externality: such definition is based on the notion of liability, and no longer

[2]In regard to the concept of mainstream implosion, and to the epistemological implications of Coase and Williamson's results, see Herscovici (2015).

on the subjective theory of value. Williamson (2002) demonstrates that, in regard to the assets specificities, the market is not systematically the most efficient mechanism.

In his analysis of the "lemon market," Akerlof (1970) refutes the hypothesis of the homogeneity of goods. He states that there are two types of sellers—honest and dishonest—and that one price may be determined by various qualities. Opportunistic behaviors and positive and negative externalities are analyzed with respect to supply:

$$p = \varphi(q_1, q_2, \ldots, q_n) \tag{2}$$

(p as price and q_n as quality l). To delet such space in regard to qn

Regarding the hypothesis that the quality of goods remains constant, additional studies (Salop 1976) have demonstrated that the dispersion of prices generates information imperfections. In this case, information becomes costly. Consumers will compare the information cost (assimilated to a marginal cost) with the possibility of obtaining the same good for a lower price. If this cost is higher than the difference in prices, the consumer will not buy the information. Therefore, several prices will correspond to the same quality. The dispersion of prices and information imperfections causes the same good to be sold for different prices, which is contrary to the law of the single price and to the homogeneity postulate.

$$p_1, p_2, \ldots, p_n = \varphi(q) \tag{3}$$

The works of Grossman and Stiglitz (1976, 1980) and Stiglitz (1987) expand the study of mechanisms arising from the existence of information imperfections, favoring components of demand:

a. The refutation of the efficient markets hypothesis was initially formulated by Grossman and Stiglitz (1976) and can be summarized by the following relationships:

$$E_1 = U_1 - p_1 - c_1 \tag{4}$$

$$E_2 = U_2 - p_2 - c_2 \tag{5}$$

where E is the expected net surplus of the consumer, U is the expected total utility and p and c are the price of goods and services and the cost paid for information, respectively. Index 1 refers to uninformed consumers, and index 2 refers to informed ones.

This mechanism can be interpreted as follows: in equilibrium, $E_1 = E_2$, that is, $U_1 - (p_1 + c_1) = U_2 - (p_2 + c_2)$. When c_2 and c_1 are higher than 0, competitive equilibrium does not exist because there is no single price.[3] In a case of competitive equilibrium, the surplus expected by uninformed consumers is equal to the surplus expected by informed consumers; $p_1 - p_2$ is compensated by $c_2 - c_1$. *Uninformed consumers benefit from positive externalities produced by informed consumers, and the equilibrium is competitive.*

The paradox of the hypothesis of efficient markets can be formulated as follows: for markets to be efficient, the price system must disclose free information from informed agents to uninformed agents. However, ex-post, the net surplus of informed agents is equal to that of uninformed agents. In this case, market efficiency and the corresponding Pareto optimum are incompatible with the hypothesis of microeconomic rationality. Why would agents buy information if the price system disclosed free qualitative information to uninformed agents?

The solution proposed by Grossman and Stiglitz is premised on the fact that the *net surplus of informed agents is higher than that of uninformed agents*; this solution can be formalized as follows:

$$E_2 = U_2 - (p_2 + c_2) > E_1 = U_1 - (p_1 + c_1) \qquad (6)$$

with $p_1 > p_2, c_2 > c_1$ and $U_2 > U_1$.

An informational rent corresponds to an economic rent. *This situation is incompatible with the Pareto optimum* because the utility gain of informed agents corresponds to the utility loss of uninformed agents. Rather, a modification of auxiliary hypotheses produces results that are incompatible with the hard core.

[3]Stiglitz (2003, p. 13) considers the principles of neoclassical economics to include "the law of the single price."

Additional studies by Stiglitz (for example, 1987) provide a more in-depth understanding of this type of approach, demonstrating that the quality of a good or service is directly related to the price. This type of analysis is generally applied to labor and credit market dynamics. Such mechanisms may be expressed by the following relationship:

$$q = \varphi(p) \tag{7}$$

with $\varphi' > 0$.

In this case, markets are rationed, and they do not reach the equilibrium position. For example, in initial unemployment conditions, the labor supply is higher than the demand: the neoclassical solution consists of a reduction in the real wages rate to restore equilibrium and reach a condition of full employment. The concept of efficiency wage clearly demonstrates that the quality of labor (i.e., its productivity) directly depends on its price, and labor demand depends on this quality. In an initial period of unemployment, a falling wage rate translates into a decline in the quality of labor and consequently a decline in demand. A cumulative process appears, and the hypothesis of market clearing is no longer verified. The flexibility of wages does not allow for a return to an equilibrium position. This is incompatible with the main GE results, i.e., with a convergence to an equilibrium position, and with the fact that this position is characterized by market clearing and full employment.

References

Akerlof, G. 1970. The Market for "Lemons": Qualitative Uncertainty and the Market Mechanism. *Quarterly Journal of Economics* 89: 488–500.

Arrow, Kenneth J. 1974a. Limited Knowledge and Economic Analysis. *American Economic Review* 64 (1) (March): 1–10.

———. 1974b. General Economic Equilibrium: Purpose, Analytic Techniques, Collective Choice. *The American Economic Review* 64 (3) (June): 253–272.

Backhouse, Roger E. 2004. Introduction. In *New Directions in Economic Methodology*, ed. Roger E. Backhouse, 1–26. Taylor & Francis e-Library. New York: Routledge.

Barrère, Alain. 1985. Le projet keynésien. In *Keynes aujourd'hui: théories et politiques.* Paris: Economica.

Barzel, Yoram. 1997. *Economic Analysis of Property Rights*. Cambridge: Cambridge University Press.
Bidard, Christian. 2014. The Ricardian Rent Theory Two Centuries After. Document de travail Working Paper 2014-54, Université de Paris Ouest Nanterre la Défense.
Blaug, Mark. 1976. Kuhn Versus Lakatos *or* Paradigms Versus Research Programmes in the History of Economics. In *Method and Appraisal in Economics*, ed. J. Spiro, 149–198. Latsis: Cambridge University Press.
Bowles, Samuel, and Herbert Gintis. 1993. The Revenge of Homo Economicus: Contested Exchange and the Revival of Political Economy. *The Journal of Economic Perspectives* 7 (1): 83–102.
Braudel, Fernand. 1985. *La dynamique du capitalisme*. Paris: Champs Flammarion.
Burgenmeier, B. 1994. The Misperception of Walras. *The American Economic Review* 84 (1) (March): 342–352.
Chick, Victoria. 2004. On Open Systems. *Brazilian Journal of Political Economy* 24 (1) (janeiro–março): 3–16.
Chick, V., and S. Dow. 2001. Formalism, Logic and Reality: A Keynesian Analysis. *Cambridge Journal of Economics* 25: 705–721.
Clark, J.M. 1891. Distribution as Determined by a Law of Rent. *Quarterly Journal of Economics* 5 (April): 289–318.
Coase, Ronald. 1960. The Problem of Social Cost. *Journal of Law and Economics* 3: 1–43.
———. 1988. *The Firm, the Market and the Law*. The University of Chicago Press.
Colander, David. 2000. The Death of Neoclassical Economics. *Journal of the History of Economic Thought* 22 (2): 127–143.
Dvoskin, Ariel, and Saverio M. Fratini. 2016. On the Samuelson-Etula Master Function and the Capital Controversy. *The European Journal of the History of Economic Thought* 23 (6): 1032–1058. https://doi.org/10.1080/09672567.2016.1186920.
Friedman, Milton. 1974. Comments on the Critics. In *Milton Friedman's Monetary Framework: A Debate with His Critics*, ed. R.J. Gordon. Chicago: University of Chicago Press.
———. 2009. *The Methodology of Positive Economic*. Cambridge: Cambridge University Press.
Grossman, S.J., and J.E. Stiglitz. 1976. Information and Competitive Price System. *The American Economic Review* 66 (2) (May): 246–253.
———. 1980. On the Impossibility of Informationally Efficient Markets. *The American Economic Review* 70 (3) (June): 393–408.

Hands, D. Wade. 2004. The Sociology of Scientific Knowledge: Some Thought on the Possibilities. In *New Directions in Economic Methodology*, ed. Roger E. Backhouse, 76–110. Taylor & Francis e-Library. New York: Routledge.
———. 2013. Mark Blaug on the Normativity of Welfare Economics. *Erasmus Journal for Philosophy and Economics* 6 (3, Special Issue) (Winter): 1–25.
Harris, Donald. 1978. *Capital Accumulation and Income Distribution*. Stanford, CA: Standford University Press.
Hausman, Daniel M. 2004. Kuhn, Lakatos and the Character of Economics. In *New Directions in Economic Methodology*, ed. Roger E. Backhouse. Taylor & Francis e-Library. New York: Routledge.
Herscovici, Alain. 2002. *Dinâmica Macroeconômica: uma interpretação a partir de Marx e de Keynes*. São Paulo: EDUC/EDUFES.
———. 2006. A teoria dos fundos de empréstimos: um estudo dos modelos agregados neoclássico e keynesiano. *Análise Econômica* (UFRGS) 46: 109–122.
———. 2015. A Economia Neoclássica: uma análise lakatosiana. *Revista de Economia Política (Impresso)* 35: 10–31.
Hicks, J.R. 1937. Mr. Keynes and the "Classics": A Suggested Interpretation. *Econometrica* 5 (2) (April): 147–159.
Hutchison, T.W. 2004. Ends and Means in the Methodology of Economics. In *New Directions in Economic Methodology*, ed. Roger E. Backhouse, 27–34. Taylor & Francis e-Library. New York: Routledge.
Keynes, John Maynard. 2009 [1936]. *The General Theory of Employment, Interest and Money*. New York: Classic Books America.
Kuhn, Thomas S. 1991/1962. *A estrutura das revoluções científicas*. São Paulo: Editora Perspectiva.
Lakatos, Imre. 1970. History of Science and Its Rational Reconstructions. *Proceedings of the Biennial Meeting of the Philosophy of Science Association* 1970: 91–136.
———. 1978. *The Methodology of Scientific Research Programs*, vol. 1. Philosophical Papers, ed. John Worral and Gregory Currie. Cambridge: Cambridge University Press.
Latsis, Spiro J. 1976. A Research Programme in Economics. In *Method and Appraisal in Economics*, ed. J. Spiro, 1–42. Latsis: Cambridge University Press.
Lisboa, Marcos. 1988. A miséria da crítica heterodoxa. *Revista de Economia Contemporânea n.3*, UFRJ.

Mankiw, N.G. 1985. Small Menu Costs and Large Business Cycles: A Macroeconomic Model of Monopoly. *The Quarterly Journal of Economics* 100 (2): 529–538.
Marcuzzo, Maria Cristina, and Annalisa Rosselli. 2011. Sraffa and His Arguments Against 'Marginism'. *Cambridge Journal of Economics* 35: 219–231.
Martins, Nuno Ornela. 2013. *The Cambridge Contribution to the Revival of Classical Political Economy*. New York: Routledge.
Orléan, André. 2011. *L'empire de la valeur. Refonderl'Économie* [The empire of value. Rebuilding the Economy]. Paris: Éditions du Seuil.
Pasinetti, L. 1997. The Marginal Efficiency of Investment. In *A "Second Edition" of the General Theory-Vol. 1*, ed. G.C. Harcourt and P.A. Riach, 198–218. Routledge: London and New York.
Petri, Fabio. 1998. The "Sraffian" Critique of Neoclassical Economics: Some Recent Developments. *Revista da Sociedade Brasileira de Economia Política* (3) (dezembro de 1998), Rio de Janeiro: 5–44.
Ricardo, David. 1821. *On the Principles of Political Economy and Taxation*, 3rd edn. Ontario: Batoche Book 2001.
Salop, Steve. 1976. Information and Monopolistic Competition. *The American Economic Review* 66 (2) (May): 240–245 (Papers and Proceedings of the Eighty-Eighth Annual Meeting of the American Economic Association).
Sen, Amartya. 1982. *Choice, Welfare and Measurement*. Oxford: Blackwell.
Stigler, George J. 1961. The Economics of Information. *The Journal of Political Economy* 69 (3) (June): 213–225.
Stiglitz, Joseph E. 1987. The Causes and Consequences of the Dependence of Quality on Price. *Journal of Economic Literature* XXV (March): 1–48.
———. 1994. *Whiter Socialism?* Cambridge, MA: MIT Press.
———. 2003. Information and the Change in the Paradigm in Economics, Part 1. *American Economist* 48 (1) (Fall): 6–26.
———. 2011. Rethinking Macroeconomics: What Failed and How to Repair It. *Journal of the European Economic Association* 9 (4) (August): 591–645.
Weintraub, R. 1985. Appraising General Equilibrium Analysis. *Economics and Philosophy* 1: 23–37.
Wicksteed, P.H. 1914. The Scope and Method of Political Economy in the Light of the 'Marginal Theory' of Value and Distribution. *Economic Journal* 24: 1–23.
Williamson, Oliver. 2002. The Theory of the Firm as Governance Structure: From Choice to Contract. *Journal of Economic Perspectives* 16 (3) (Summer): 171–195.

4

Ricardo, Keynes and Stiglitz: The Epistemological Convergences

1 Capital Historicity

1.1 Capital Heterogeneity: The Epistemological Convergences

Heterogeneity is defined from two temporal dimensions: the first one is related to the evaluation of a stock composed by heterogeneous capitals, in a specific point of time. Nevertheless, as we have to evaluate various kinds of capitals, i.e., investments realized in different periods of the past, an updating process is necessary; we have to update these capitals to express its values in regard to the current variables: Sraffa will update the capital (dated labor) from the current profit rate, Keynes from the current long-term expectations, and Stiglitz from the current information asymmetries.

The second dimension is related to the comparison of the value of some stock of capital in different periods. Time appears twice in such mechanism: to evaluate the value of the stock in *t*, and to compare the value of the stock in *t* and in *t + 1*.

A. Herscovici, *Essays on the Historicity of Capital*,
https://doi.org/10.1007/978-3-030-14838-6_4

Such mechanism is intrinsically dynamic, as, as wrote Schumpeter (1954, vol. III, p. 506), it concerns "(...) a relationship between economic quantities located at different moments of time." On the contrary, a static method is characterized by the study of relationships between economic elements related to the same periods.

We can conclude that the Ricardian and the Keynesian methods are twice dynamic. Consequently, the neoclassical conception of capital is, by nature, static, as value is equivalent to a quantity of capital, and constant over time.

For such reasons, *the different forms of heterogeneity of capital translate into an intrinsic historical analysis*: heterogeneity is defined by the temporal structure (Ricardo and Sraffa), by the long-run expectations (Keynes), or by the information asymmetries (Akerlof 1970; Grossman and Stiglitz 1976, 1980). *History implies that these variables change over time, so that their values change too*; from such reasoning, constant value are equivalent to the absence of change. All neoclassical analysis universalizes and reifies concept of capital.

1.2 The Cambridge Controversy: Simple Formalization

1.2.1 A First Approach

The main theoretical results of neo-Ricardian theory may be synthesized from the following example[1]: we consider two commodities A and B, each produced by capital C_A and C_B, and some quantity of labor, L_A and L_B. Obviously, C is expressed in labor quantity, in terms of indirect labor:

$$L_A + C_A = L_B + C_B \tag{1}$$

In regard to the Ricardian labor theory, relation (1) implies that A value is equal to B value:

$$A = B \tag{2}$$

[1] In respect to a complete presentation, see Cohen and Harcourt (2003).

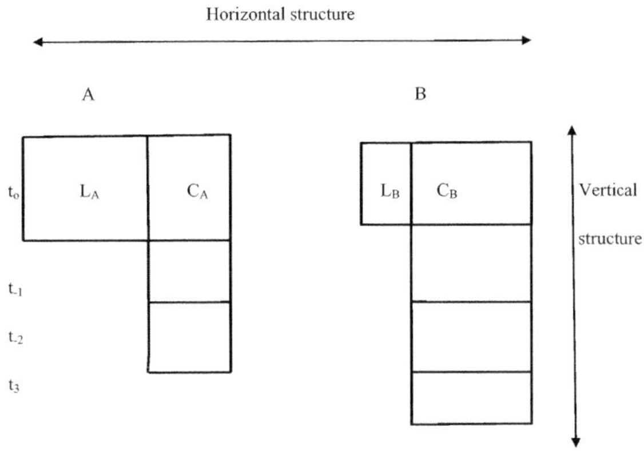

Fig. 1 The Ricardian value theory

Capital is conceived as labor "spent" in the past, as a "*round-about method of production*" (Hayek 2009); it must get an economic return every period. *The dated labor is evaluated, in each period, based on the current profit rate* (Fig. 1).

Relation (1) is verified only when the horizontal and the vertical structures are the same for *A* and *B*. It will be also verified when the profit rate is nil; nevertheless, such solution is a no-sense, from an economic perspective. As there are no reasons for the horizontal and vertical structure being the same for the two commodities, *A* value is different from *B* value.

If we consider a high profit rate, *B* value will be greater than *A* value. As the wages rate increases (which means that profit rate decreases), *B* value will decrease in relation to *A* value: dated labor is updated from a smaller rate and current labor from a higher rate.

We can write:

$$V_B = \gamma \cdot V_A \tag{3}$$

equivalent to:

$$\gamma = V_B / V_A \tag{4}$$

$$\gamma = \varphi(w) \tag{5}$$

$$\gamma' < 0.$$

1.2.2 The Reswitching of Techniques

The reswitching of techniques reveals the logical implications related to this mechanism (Fig. 2).

Between 0 and r_1, when w is high (r is low), technique II will be chosen. This means that, for a low price of capital, technique II is the more capitalistic. Between r_1 and $r_{2,}$ technique I will be chosen; there is a switching of techniques. So, we can affirm, without ambiguity, that II is a more capitalistic technique, and I the less capitalistic. However, between r_2 and r_3, II is chosen one more time, when r increases; this is called the reswitching of techniques. Such choice implies that II is a less capitalistic technique. From 0 to r_3, II is, at the same time, the most and the least capitalistic technique.

Obviously, this highlights a logical incoherency; such incoherency is explained by the refutation of the monotonic relation between r and k, the ratio capital/labor; the value of some quantity of capital changes when the distributive variables change, as well as the ratio capital/labor. It is the reason why "(…) a fall in the rate of profit, which, in a neoclassical approach, is deemed to favor the introduction of more

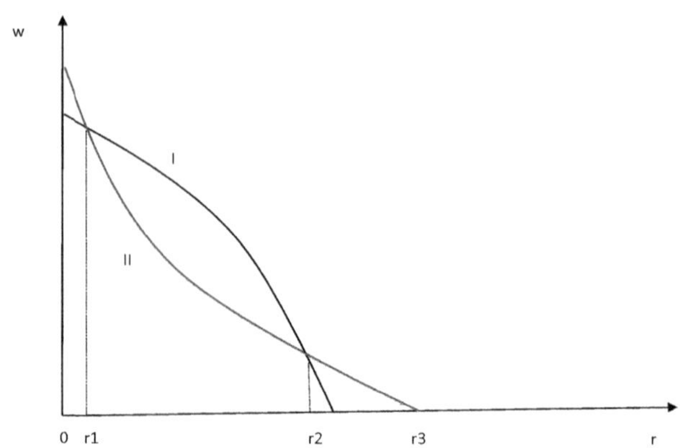

Fig. 2 The reswitching of techniques

capitalistic techniques, may not lead to an increase in the product per head" (Bidard 2014, p. 10). The *reswitching of techniques is the direct manifestation of this mechanism,* i.e., of such modalities of determination of the value of some amount of capital.

1.3 Keynesian and Neo-Ricardian Theories and the Criticism of Neoclassical Framework

1.3.1 The Historical Dimension

Such result is totally incompatible with the universalist axiom: as, in the long term, distributive variables change, the value of some stock of capital cannot be constant. In this respect, Kaldor noted that, at aggregate level, the capital coefficient depends on the interest rate (1955–1956, p. 98): capital value cannot be measured independently of distributive variables.

Theoretically, the product is relative to a specific period and represents a *flow:* it is a "short-run" variable which concerns only the current period. The total capital value is a *stock* related to the "long run"; its evaluation is related to various periods, i.e., to various generations of capital. If we may consider that it is possible to evaluate, i.e., to quantify the product, the problem related to the quantification of the stock is more complex; the reevaluation of the capital stock value must be related to the current conditions and, consequently, changes over time.

The ratio capital/product is generally interpreted in the following manner: if, for example, this ratio is equal to 6, capital stock is the equivalent of six years of national income. Such interpretation implies that the value of capital was reevaluated from the current variables, to compare two magnitudes related to the same period. It is not possible, as Piketty does (2014, p. 108), to evaluate an aggregate stock of capital from its current market price: its volatility is very high and its current value is not representative of its "long-term value."

Facing this problem, Keynes evaluates the product evolution from the labor quantities employed (TG, p. 37). On other hand, Keynes defines the supply price of capital in the following way:

$$Po = \frac{\sum Qi}{(1+e)^n} \quad (6)$$

(Po as supply price, Qi as the expected product at period i and e as the capital marginal efficiency).

The investment expected product of each period is updated from the current rate, i.e., from the marginal efficiency of capital that moves over time (see Chapter 6). At this respect, Keynes observes that the marginal efficiency of capital "(…) is defined in terms of the expectation of yield and of the *current supply price of the capital-asset*" (GT, p. 112, emphasis added). Then, he adds that it does not depend "(…) on the historical result of what an investment has yielded on its original cost if we look back on its record after its life is over" (idem.). In such mechanism, the value of capital, i.e., investment, is updated at each period, from the current long-term expectations.

The Ricardian theory of differential rent allows formulating the same conclusion. We can consider two qualities of land and two periods; in the first period, the corn value is determined by the labor quantity spent on the land of best quality, and in the second, by the labor quantity spent on the land of worst quality. The corn value is reevaluated at each period and determined by the labor quantity spent on worst quality land; consequently, the corn value increases as it becomes necessary to cultivate land of inferior quality. This theory is a parable (Harcourt 1972) that poses the problem of the heterogeneity of production factors and of its measure at an aggregate level.

We can affirm that the epistemological convergences between the Keynesian and the neo-Ricardian SRP are founded on two basic elements: the first one is related to the historicity of capital and the second one, consequently, on the refutation of the neoclassical program. In regard to the second element, we agree with Martins when this author argues that "The Cambridge controversies in the theory of capital show us a moment where Keynesians, Kaleckians and Sraffians stand united in the rejection of neoclassical economics" (2013, p. 17).

1.3.2 Labor Value Theory and Ricardian Economics

1.3.2.1 We must formulate the problem in the following terms: is the Ricardian Economy intrinsically dependent on the labor value theory, and do such labor values allow determining relative prices? Various neo-Ricardian authors refute these sentences for the following reasons:

As seen in the last subsection, from a logical point of view, the amount of labor allows explaining the relative prices in two specific situations: when the rate of profit is nil,[2] or when all the sectors have the same horizontal and vertical structures. These situations are specific, and cannot be considered as general cases. When such conditions are not verified, the labor value theory does not explain, from a purely logical point of view, the relative prices.

At this respect, Ricardo in the Principles, after having highlighted the limits of his theory of embodied labor, considers that this theory nevertheless allows providing a "satisfactory" tool to measure "(...) all the great variations which take place in the variations of the relative value of commodities to be produced by the greater or less quantity of labor which may be required from time to time to produce them" (1821, p. 27).

This allows raising the problem related to the role of the labor value theory in the Ricardian Economics: does such value theory provide a way to measure and to quantify relative prices from the quantity of labor? At this respect, Sraffa affirms that:

It is the *whole* process of production that must be called "human labor," and thus causes all product and all values. Marx and Ricardo used "labor" in two different senses: the above, and that of *one* of the factors of production ("hours of labor" or "quantity of labor" has a meaning only in the latter sense). It is by confusing the two senses that they got mixed up and said that value is proportional to quantity of labor (in second sense), whereas they ought to have said that it is due to *human labor* (in first sense: *a non measurable quantity, or rather not a quantity at all*) (cited by Kurz and Salvadori 2014, p. 64; emphases added).

---

[2]See Kurz and Salvadori (2014, p. 25).

If we compare Ricardo and Smith's theory, we can formulate the same conclusion. The commanded labor theory is defined by the quantity of labor that a commodity A can purchase when exchanged with B. But this definition implies that this quantity is defined by the labor quantity embodied in B. *We can conclude that while the theory of commanded labor is linked to the measurement of value, the embodied labor theory explains the cause of value* (Martins 2013, p. 4). If we accept this conclusion, we can argue that Ricardo's labor value theory may not be interpreted from the measurement conception of labor value theory.

The labor value theory has to face the problem related to the absence of a standard commodity: if we compare all commodities with the labor, the value of the labor must be constant. On the other hand, if we define the value of labor from the value of commodities which correspond to the worker's consumption, we define the value of labor by the value of the labor embodied in such commodities (Kurz and Salvadori 2010, p. 12).

We must observe that Marx, from his resolution of the 'transformation problem,' clarified partially this problem:

(i) Contrarily to Ricardo, he demonstrates that, at the sectorial level, when the equalization of the sectorial rate of profit is realized, the production prices have to be quantitatively different from the labor quantities; such difference is explained from the different organic composition of capital in the different sectors. Marx went beyond Ricardo as he demonstrated that, at the sectorial level, price must be quantitatively different from values, and that such difference is not random, but determined from the labor values.
(ii) At the aggregate level, the problem may be formulated in the following terms: labor values must be equal to production prices and, simultaneously surplus value to profits.

The neo-Ricardian resolutions may be enounced in the following manner: these two relations will be verified only when the organic composition of the third sector (which produces the goods that the capitalists consume) has the same organic composition of capital as the average one of the whole economy. If such condition is not realized, we can verify only one of these two relations.

From a Marxian perspective, we must consider that only the first relation is verified, i.e., the whole prices are equal to the whole labor values. Such choice highlights the *logical anteriority* of labor value in regard to production prices, and we can justify the difference between profits and surplus value (Herscovici 2002). Once again, the problem consists in knowing if the quantities of labor allow measuring the prices, or whether such relations means that the source of the value is the labor. In other words, what is the nature of the deterministic relation between labor values and prices?

1.3.2.2 Keynes reached the same conclusion: in regard the heterogeneity of goods and services, he argues that "(…) the community's output of goods and services (…) cannot be measured, strictly speaking, except in certain special cases, as for example when all the items of one output are included in the same proportions in another output" (GT, p. 33).

We can note that two fundamental elements appear in such sentence: the heterogeneity of goods (and consequently of capitals) and the Ricardian/Sraffaian approach which allowed designing the reswitching of techniques.

On the other hand, Keynes will measure the increase of output by the labor quantity:

> When, for purpose of description or rough comparison, we wish to speak of an increase of output, we must rely on the general assumption that the amount of employment associated with some given capital equipment will be a *satisfactory* index in the amount of resultant input—the two being presumed to increase and decrease together, *though not in a definite numerical proportion.* (GT, p. 35 emphases added)

Within a Ricardian perspective, Keynes points out the same problems related to "imperfections" of the labor quantity as value measurement, and adopts the same *démarche*: he will "(…) measure changes in the current output by reference to the number of hours paid for (…)" (GT, p. 37); and, as Ricardo did, he considers that labor is the source of economic value. He "(…) sympathized (…) with the "pre-classical" doctrine that everything is produced by labor (…) and by the result of past labor (…) (GT, pp. 213–214).

1.3.2.3 *So, is it possible to affirm that the labor theory value is not necessary to prove the Sraffaian results?* The Sraffaian resolution of the transformation problem allows enunciating similar results: the system in prices does not depend on the system in labor value; the two systems are disconnected (Herscovici 2002). Nevertheless, we need a common substance to aggregate heterogeneous goods and capitals: for this purpose, we can use any common elements, as the weight, the length, and so on. We do not need to determine previously the variables in labor value to deduce the variables in prices[3]; it is the reason why I qualified such resolution as formal (Herscovici 2002).

But what is the economic meaning of this choice? Such choice implies eliminating the historical dimension and adopting the universalist thesis, as the neoclassical school did. This also means adopting a research program whose contradictions were highlighted by Sraffa and not resolved by its own participants. Even if, according to certain writings, it seems that Sraffa rejected the labor value theory, such theory is a fundamental element of the entire neo-Ricardian framework: it allows formalizing the reswitching of techniques and determining the modalities of measurement of the capital and its historical changes.

I conceive Ricardo and Sraffa's theory as intrinsically historicist: consequently, and contrarily to Kurz and Salvadori's position (2010, p. 9), Sraffa's framework cannot be founded on "(…) physical data concerning production condition and real wages (…)" and cannot adopt the substantial hypothesis.

On the other hand, we must interpret the Ricardian/Sraffaian framework from the labor value theory, knowing that it constitutes an imperfect tool of measurement, i.e., a *proxy*. This choice allows using an economic (I mean social and historical, in opposition to natural) common substance to measure goods and capitals.

The Cambridge controversy may be expressed in the following terms: on the one hand, the neoclassical position ignores voluntarily this controversy, and continues, from a physical conception of capital, using

[3]The mathematical systems designed by Bortkiewicz (1959) and Winternitz (1948) allow formulating this conclusion. In this respect, see Herscovici (2002).

production function (Cobb-Douglas, or CES functions) and measuring capital in quantities (Dvoskin and Fratini 2016). On the other hand, the Ricardian/Keynesian approach, from an imperfect measurement tool, demonstrates that the construction of such function is incoherent.

What is the best choice? (a) To ignore the critic, and to continue as if such controversy never existed, as the mainstream did or (b) to design an alternative conception intrinsically historical, even knowing its limits? From a Lakatosian approach, the second option looks more satisfactory. As argued Lakatos, the progressive character of some SRP is determined in a relative manner; from a comparison between the neoclassical SRP and the neo-Ricardian one, the latter may be considered progressive.

2 Keynes and Stiglitz: Expectations, Value and Social Relations

2.1 The Self-Referential Value

2.1.1 The Newspaper Competition Parable

The concept of self-referential value was designed by Keynes in the GT, from the parable of the newspapers competition whose winner is the competitor whose choice more nearly corresponds to the real choice made by the "public opinion." Such parable is used to describe the mechanism that corresponds to the financial speculation, and to explain why some agents realize gains.

> (…) the price being awarded to the competitor whose choice most nearly corresponds to the average preferences of the competitors as a whole; so that each competitor has to pick, not those faces which he himself finds prettiest, but those faces which he thinks likeliest to catch the fancy of other competitors, all of whom are looking at the problem from the same point of view. (…) We have reached the third degree where we devote our intelligences to anticipating what average opinion expects the average opinion to be. (GT, p. 130)

Each individual may elaborate expectations related to the intrinsic value of the asset and determines its fundamental value (the face that is, for him, the most beautiful one). Nevertheless, there is no objective reason for the market validating this specific expectation; the market only validates the average opinion. If we define as *first degree expectations* those that correspond to the face that each competitor considers the most beautiful, and *second degree expectations,* those that each competitor thinks that the market will choose, the individual that will win is the one that foresees better the expectations expressed by the majority of participants.

If each individual creates expectations from such mechanism, the market will validate the expectations related to the expectations related to the expectations of the most part of the individual; it is a *third degree expectation*.

We should also note that the way a concrete market is working implies that individual's expectations are not homogeneous; such expectations must be divergent. In a speculative market, for the exchange being realized, some individual must believe that the asset value will increase, and other that it will decrease (Grossman and Stiglitz 1980). The "majority opinion" will determine the effective tendency.

This mechanism is characterized by a *self-referential definition of value*; the value effectively validated by the market is the one that corresponds to the majority expectations. There is no constant long-term position value that market prices will reach, but value is determined by such interactions, in regard to expectations modalities of elaboration, and to mimetic behaviors. Such value is relatively stable when a specific convention is working, and changes when the convention changes (GT, p. 126). *Value is not an imminent property of the assets*; *on the contrary, value is created and modified from such social interactions, i.e., from such modalities of elaboration of expectations and beliefs.*

Speculative bubbles may be analyzed from such perspective. Given that the value is no longer determined by reference to fixed parameters, but due to self-realizable expectations, a cumulative process may appear and develop from some determinate *convention.* Such process may include upward or downward expectations: the speculative bubble will remain as such convention remains. Fluctuations are not limited by the divergence from the fundamental value because such fundamental value does not exist.

Contrary to neoclassical analysis (more specifically to rational expectations analysis), there is no intrinsic value that constitutes the regulatory variable from which the market prices will oscillate: on the contrary, value is determined by these self-realizable expectations and by the individual behaviors; in other words, *there is an endogenous determination of value.*

This approach is intrinsically different from the analysis that rational expectations theory makes of speculative bubbles: first, there is not fundamental value to regulate and to limit the prices variations. Second, expectations are heterogeneous; not all individuals have the same expectations.

In the absence of regulatory variables, i.e., of fundamental value, such markets are particularly unstable: consequently, the value of a stock of heterogeneous capitals varies in a significant way in the different periods considered.

2.1.2 The Concept of Relational Economics

The refutation of the substantive hypothesis explains why it is necessary to provide alternative explanation of the determinant of value: these explanations will focalize on the relationships between individual.

As seen before, speculative fluctuations are the product of such relationships: the speculator gain comes from the fact that he anticipates "(…) the base of conventional valuation a few months hence (…)" (GT, p. 129). This framework was developed by Grossman and Stiglitz (1976, 1980): in regard to financial market, in Chapter 7, I will demonstrate that informed agents realize gains because non informed agents realize losses. Value is produced by the combination of mimetic behaviors and asymmetric information.

The price system does not convey all qualitative information and there is a strong uncertainty in regard to quality. The efficiency wages theory, for example, demonstrates that the quality of the labor depends directly on its price. Consequently, there is a positive correlation between wages and demand for labor; this is an atypical demand function. Then, labor quality depends on the worker's ex-post behavior.

In this sense, it is possible to speak in relational economics. Finally, the homogeneity hypothesis is not more verified: quality is not constant neither can be considered as an intrinsic characteristic of the asset (or commodity), but depends on the behavior of the supplier.

Relational Economics highlights the fact that asset value is the result of interactions between individual: *value (and capital value) is produced, in an endogenous way, by the market.* Once again, we can see that the possibility to measure capital and its evolutions in the long run in quantities implies that such relations must be permanent. And they are not: first, the absence of a fundamental value translates into a high volatility of such market; second, an average value in the long term is not representative of the speculative dimension of such markets, in regard to the *high temporal dispersion of such value.*

2.2 The Refutation of Nomenclature Hypothesis: Grossman and Stiglitz

2.2.1 The Quality Problem

In the neoclassical framework, the characteristics of the goods and services are the same for all consumers: quality is determined and constant. There is an objective and ex-ante determination of the utility; *there is not uncertainty relative to qualities.*

The homogeneity hypothesis adopted by the neoclassical economics allows defining the *objective characteristics* of goods and assets, independently from social, historical and economic variables (Orléan 2011, p. 87); this means defining the intrinsic value, in its qualitative dimensions. Such value is determined independently from price and from relationship between agents on the market. It is possible to justify such hypotheses from the following reasons: (a) the intrinsic qualitative characteristics of the goods are known by the agents; or (b) the agents share beforehand a common knowledge that allows knowing such characteristics; but this situation is incompatible with the methodological individualism (Arrow 1986, p. 390).

The nomenclature hypothesis allows verifying the homogeneity postulate: prices convey the adequate signal for the individual to evaluate goods qualities. Quality is determined objectively, and does not depend on prices, on individual's behaviors, or on individual relationships.

Grossman and Stiglitz (1976, 1980) refute the homogeneity postulate; economic value is "relational." From the example of financial markets, they define two categories of agents: the informed ones and the non-informed ones. The financial assets demand depends on the quality, i.e., its expected return. Such return is evaluated from two elements: the information which allows reducing the risk, and the price. The non-informed agents deduce the expected return from the price, while the informed ones from information and price.

These information asymmetries explain the speculative cycle and the variations of the assets value. *In the first moment*, the informed agents buy the assets that present the higher return; *in the second moment*, as a result of the increased demand in the previous period, prices increase. The non-informed agents deduce that the quality assets increased and their demand increases; on the contrary, in relation to the price increase, the informed agents demand decreases.

Such process becomes *cumulative* from the moment that the increase of the non-informed agents demand is higher than the informed agents demand decrease; these conditions are verified when most part of the agents is not informed and/or the information cost is high (Grossman and Stiglitz 1980). These asymmetries explain the gains realized by the informed agents: they buy the asset when its value is low and sell it when its value increases.

This analysis demonstrates that the value is determined in an endogenous manner, by the relationships among the different types of agents: the value is the result of these inter-individual relationships, of the information asymmetries and of the way expectations are elaborated.

According to Keynes, the gains are realized by the agents who anticipate before the most part the majority behavior, i.e., the future convention which will be adopted by the majority. The public opinion fails to elaborate such expectations in the right period, and, for this reason, it is harmed. *The convention is a self-referential and a cumulative mechanism.*

Information asymmetries are not defined by hiding information, or part of them; such situation would not produce the externalities that explain the gains of the informed agents. Information asymmetries consist in producing *lags* between the different kinds of agents: while the non-informed are victims of their mimetic behavior, the informed ones realize financial gains. *This kind of interrelation determines the effective asset values.*

2.2.2 Two Examples: The Labor Market and the Banking Market

From the example of labor or banking market, Stiglitz demonstrates that quality depends on the prices:

- In regard to the labor market, the higher the rate wages, the higher the labor quality, i.e., the effective labor productivity (Stiglitz 1987, p. 5). Quality is not an intrinsic quality of the commodities, but it depends on the worker's ex-post behavior; labor demand is atypical, as it increases in relation to prices.
- The same mechanism works on the banking market: the higher the interest rate that the agent accepts to get loan, the higher the risk of insolvency, and the lower the supply of funds by the bank. Such supply function is atypical too.

(a) Value depends on the information asymmetries and the relationships between individual.
(b) Prices do not convey the necessary information to evaluate the qualitative components of the goods and services; the same price variation will be interpreted in different ways by the different groups of individual.
(c) The market price system does not equilibrate markets: it does not allow realizing the market clearing, but on the contrary, the markets are *rationed.*

By refuting the homogeneity postulate, Akerlof, Grossman and Stiglitz's results are incompatible with neoclassical economics. The homogeneity postulate may be represented by the following relation:

$$p = \phi(q) \tag{7}$$

Price depends on the quality and the price system provides a perfect signal in regard to quality.

Contrarily, Stiglitz's results highlight the following relation:

$$q = \phi(p) \tag{8}$$

Quality depends on the prices; it depends on the ex-post behaviors of the individual who participate in the exchange. It is a refutation of the substantial hypothesis and of the neoclassical framework: such economy is intrinsically relational.

Akerlof's model is centered upon asymmetries between sellers and buyers (1970); asymmetries depend on the supply behavior. Grossman and Stiglitz models are focalized upon asymmetries between informed and no informed agents, i.e., upon the demand side. Such asymmetries may be represented by the following relation:

$$p = \varphi(q_1, q_2, \ldots, q_n) \tag{9}$$

As shown by (8) and (9), the homogeneity postulate is not verified.

2.3 The Example of Financial Markets: Fundamental Value Versus Social Value

2.3.1 Productive and Speculative Finance

Several statements in Chapter 12 of the GT emphasize the fact that speculative activity is, by nature, related to the short term. Keynes defines speculation as "(...) the battle of wits to anticipate the basis of conventional valuations a few months hence, rather than the prospective yields of an investment over a long term of years (...)" (GT, p. 129) and opposes short-term speculation to long-term productive investment.

When Keynes designs the investment function, he compares the marginal efficiency of capital with the interest rate. It is a *choice asset theory* as far as the entrepreneur compares the yield of the productive asset with the yield of a financial one. The return of a "productive" financial asset depends on the interest rate and not on the variation of its value; this constant yield is calculated from the initial value. On the other hand, the yield of a speculative financial asset is due to its value variations.

We can illustrate such mechanism from the example of what Keynes calls speculative motive (GT, p. 142): the agents who forecast an increase in the interest rate (the "bears") will forecast a decrease in the value of the asset. So, they will buy such asset "tomorrow" and "today" they will choose money: "today," the demand of money for speculative motive will decrease and the liquidity preference will increase. The agents who forecast a decrease in the interest rate will have the opposite behavior: "today," their demand of money for speculative motive will increase, and their liquidity preference will decrease.

If, for example, the value of a bond is initially \$100, and if the interest rate is 10%, the yield of the agent who buys the asset will be \$10 for each period. If the interest rate increases to 20%, the bond market's stability implies that the bond's value decreases to \$50: in both cases, the return will be \$10 for each period. Such stability implies the absence of a speculative dimension in the primary markets, and in the fact that such bonds will finance the productive investment. At this respect, we can speak in terms of *productive finance*.

The purchase of a financial security is justified from the moment its return during its life is equal to (or higher than) its offer price, or its fundamental value (Tirole 2016, p. 405). This long-term perspective is characterized by its stability and by the absence of a speculative dimension; liquidity is not a necessary condition for such kind of finance.

As long as the yield will be \$10 in each period, speculative activities consist in buying the asset when its value is low, and selling it when its value is high; in other words, from a speculative perspective, the return of such activities depends on the variations of the asset values, by forecasting, before most agents, the interest rate variations. Liquidity is an important feature: it allows negotiating these assets in the secondary markets (GT, p. 140): "(…) the existence of an organized market gives an opportunity for wide fluctuations in liquidity-preference due to the speculative-motive" (GT, p. 142). *These speculative activities are characterized by its instability, by the uncertainty in regard to interest rate variations, and by the disconnection in regard to the productive activities*: it is the reason why I will call it *speculative finance.*[4]

2.3.2 Some Macroeconomic Implications

According to Keynes' analysis, each asset depends on three attributes: q as the expected yield, c as the carrying cost, l as the liquidity-premium, and a as the expected appreciation of the asset in terms of itself (GT, p. 191). The return of each asset is equal to $(q - c + 1 + a)$. If we consider, for example, three assets, a productive one, a speculative/financial one and money, and if we suppose that the carrying costs are negligible, the stock equilibrium implies that the return of each asset is equal:

$$q_1 + a_1 = a_2 = l_3 \tag{10}$$

q_1 as the expected return of the productive investment and a_1 as its supply price. Assets 1 is a productive asset, asset 2 a bond and asset 3, money.

From (10), we can compare three assets:

(a) The yield of the productive investment is equal to $q_1 + a_{1,}$ and it is essentially determined in the long run.
(b) In regard to the speculative finance, the financial investment yield is determined by $a_{2.}$
(c) The money yield is equal to its liquidity premium, i.e., to $l_{3.}$

Equilibrium is realized when (10) is verified.

When the productive investment yield is higher than other assets yield, its demand increases, as well as its production, and its marginal efficiency decreases until it is verified (10). Nevertheless, such mechanism does not work in regard to a financial asset: in the financial cycle dynamics, under determinate conditions, its value increases together with its demand.

[4]Orléan (2011, p. 267) enunciates the same observations.

The financialization process appears and grows when the financial assets yields are higher than those of the productive investment. The short-run expectations that determine the speculative logic determine the average yields for all kind of assets, including the productive ones.

(i) As the Stock Exchange market realizes daily revaluations of the assets, short-run speculators' expectations "(…) exert a decisive influence on the rate of current investment." (GT, p. 125). *Financial governance* appears and grows; the productive investment yields "(…) are determined by the average expectation of those who deal on the Stock Exchange." (GT, p. 125). During a financial bubble, when prospective yields are high, the demand transfer from productive sector to the financial one translates into a decrease in productive investment, as long as various productive investments cannot reach such return.
(ii) Finally, as financial assets production elasticity is very low, such transfer implies a decrease in total employment level and a rent concentration in favor of speculators. In a Keynesian approach, the development of financial markets implies a decrease in the expenditure multiplier; the macroeconomic effects of economic policies are diminished.

We can describe this mechanism in the following manner: from a Keynesian perspective, the productive investment function may be designed by:

$$I = \varphi(e - r) \tag{11}$$

where I is the investment, e as the capital marginal efficiency and r is the yield of speculative financial asset.

The higher r, the lower I, as well as the product and the employment levels; speculative activities push up the rate of return and translate into a decrease of the investment, the product and the employment level.

2.3.3 The Effects Upon the Multiplier

Keynes differentiates industries in regard to their employment and production elasticity. Such elasticity measures the employment and production variations induced by an initial variation of Effective Demand. The employment elasticity may be defined in the following way:

$$e_{\mathrm{er}} = \frac{dNr/Nr}{dDwr/Dwr} = \frac{dNr}{dWr} \cdot \frac{Dwr}{Nr} \tag{12}$$

And the production elasticity by the following equation:

$$e_{\mathrm{ep}} = \frac{dOr/Or}{dDwr/Dwr} = \frac{dOr}{dDWr} \cdot \frac{Dwr}{Or} \tag{13}$$

where *Nr* is the volume of employment, *Dwr* is the effective demand, *Or* is the supply and *t* is the temporal index.

On the one hand, the low production elasticity may be explained by the heterogeneity of the goods and of the assets. The producers act as monopolies, and it is the reason why an increase in the demand of such assets will result in a price adjustment, and not in quantity adjustment. The supply of such assets is intrinsically limited (Tirole 2016, p. 407); if it were not, when the demand increases, the prices would increase; in the next period, the supply would increase and the prices would decrease: in such case, price variations would be limited, as well as speculation.

The multiplier will be low for two reasons: first, the inequality of the rent distribution implies a high marginal propensity to save. Secondly, the heterogeneity of assets corresponds to low production elasticity.

On the other hand, Keynes affirms that "Moreover, if the increased demand is directed to products with a relatively low elasticity of employment, a larger proportion of it will swell the incomes of entrepreneurs (…)" (GT, p. 247). The development of such markets translates into higher unemployment, higher speculators' rent and, consequently, higher rent inequalities (Dávila-Fernández and Oreiro 2016).

Final Remarks: The Epistemological Convergences

From an epistemological perspective, we can argue that the value theory does not constitute a demarcation criterion to differentiate and characterize the different economic schools. The value theory is a hypothesis which belongs to some hard core, and which cannot be proved or refuted; some "liberal" authors do not adopt the neoclassical value theory (Hayek, for example), and, as seen, other qualified of "heterodox" do not adopt, systematically the labor value theory, as Akerlof and Stiglitz.

We can deduce that the Ricardian, Keynesian and Stiglitzian SRPs share another common epistemological characteristic: independently of the value theory, or the absence of such theory, theses SRPs emphasize the heterogeneity of capital and its economic implications. It is the reason why I consider these programs together: they highlight the historicity of the capital and, consequently, allow refuting the neoclassical mechanisms and results.

From a Ricardian or a Keynesian perspective, assuming that an aggregate quantity of capital is a constant value *implies the historical permanency of some social relationships and some modalities of expectations elaboration*. History is "immutable" and in the sense it is characterized by some fundamental and permanent components; this corresponds to the Popperian thesis.

The definition of study object itself and the design of the empirical tools depend on these premises; scarcity is conceived as a natural, and not a social and historical fact. On the contrary, the historicist thesis defines other research object for the economic sciences, other global architecture and other causalities.

I believe that one of the main elements that can define the theoretical rupture between orthodox and heterodox Economics is related to the integration or the refutation of this historical dimension: History, and more precisely Historicity, is characterized by the qualitative and quantitative evolutions of social relation, in time and in space. The refutation of such historical dimension leads to the trap of economic formalism; as Polanyi wrote, in regard to the "liberal" philosophy, it "*(…) failed so conspicuously as in its understanding of the problem of change*" (Polanyi 1992, p. 41).

References

Akerlof, G. 1970. The Market for "Lemons": Qualitative Uncertainty and the Market Mechanism. *Quarterly Journal of Economics* 89 (August): 488–500.

Arrow, Kenneth J. 1986. Rationality of Self and Others in an Economic System. *The Journal of Business* 59 (4): 385–399.

Bidard, Christian 2014. The Ricardian Rent Theory Two Centuries after, Document de travail Working Paper 2014–54, Université de Paris Ouest Nanterre la Défense.

Bortkiewicz, Ladislauss von. 1959. Essai de rectification de la construction théorique fondamentale de Marx dans le troisième livre du Capital. *Cahiers de l' ISEA* 76 (janv.): 20–36.

Cohen, Avi J., and Harcourt G.C. 2003. Whatever Happened to the Cambridge Capital Theory Controversies? *Journal of Economic Perspectives* 17 (Winter).

Dávila-Fernández, Marwiland, and José Luis Oreiro. 2016. Piketty in the Light of Pasinetti and Foley: Income Distribution, Economic Growth and Financial Fragility, *Revista de Economia Política*, São Paulo, vol. 36, nº 4 (145): 667–683, October–December/2016.

Dvoskin, Ariel, and Saverio M. Fratini. 2016. On the Samuelson–Etula Master Function and the Capital Controversy. *The European Journal of the History of Economic Thought* 23 (6): 1032–1058. https://doi.org/10.1080/09672567.2016.1186920.

Grossman, S.J., and J.E. Stiglitz. 1976. Information and Competitive Price system. *The American Economic Review* 66 (2) (May): 246–253.

———. 1980. On the Impossibility of Informationally Efficient Markets. *The American Economic Review* 70 (3) (June): 393–408.

Harcourt, G.C. 1972. *Some Cambridge Controversies in the Theory of Capital.* Cambridge: Cambridge University Press.

Hayek, F.H. 2009 [1950]. *The Pure Theory of Capital.* Auburn, AL: The Ludwig von Mises Institute.

Herscovici, Alain. 2002. *Dinâmica Macroeconômica: uma interpretação a partir de Marx e de Keynes.* São Paulo: EDUC/EDUFES.

Kaldor, Nicholas. 1955–1956. Alternative Theories of Distribution. *The Review of Economic Studies* 23 (2): 83–100.

Keynes, John Maynard. 2009 [1936]. *The General Theory of Employment, Interest and Money.* New York: Classic Books America.

Kurz, Heinz D., and N. Salvadori. 2010. Sraffa and the Labour Theory of Value. *A Few Observations. In Economic Theory and Economic Thought*, ed. John Vint, J. Stanley Metcalfe, Heinz D. Kurz, Neri Salvadori, and Paul Samuelson, 187–213. London: Routledge.

Kurz, Heinz D., and N. Salvadori. 2014. Classical Economics After Sraffa, Paper Given at the Conference "What have we learnt on Classical Economics Since Sraffa?", Université Paris Ouest Nanterre, (October): 16–17.

Martins, Nuno Ornela. 2013. *The Cambridge Contribution to the Revival of Classical Political Economy*. New York and London: Routledge.

Orléan, André. 2011. *L'empire de la valeur. Refonder l'Économie*. Paris: Éditions du Seuil.

Piketty, Thomas. 2014. *Capital in the Twenty First Century*. Cambridge, Massachusetts London, England: The Belknap Press of Harvard University Press.

Polanyi, Karl. 1992 [1944]. *The Great Transformation, La Grande Transformation. The Politic and Economic Origins of Our Time*. Boston: Beacon Press.

Ricardo, David. 1821. *On the Principles of Political Economy and Taxation*, 3rd ed. Ontario: Batoche Books 2001.

Schumpeter, Joseph A., 1983 [1954]. *Histoire de l'analyse économique. L'âge de la science—III*. Paris: Gallimard.

Stiglitz, Joseph E. 1987 The Causes and Consequences of the Dependence of Quality on Price. *Journal of Economic Literature* XXV (March): 1–48.

Tirole, Jean. 2016. *Economie du bien commun*. Paris: PUF.

Winternitz, J. 1948. Values and Prices: A Solution of the So-Called Transformation Problem. *Economic Journal* 58: 276–280.

Part II

Historicity and Economic Sciences

5

Theory of Differential Rent and Capital Heterogeneity: A Neo-Ricardian Analysis

> The question reflects the historical development of marginal productivity theory whereby, in a perfectly competitive economy and in the long-run equilibrium, the Malthusian and Ricardian theory of rent was extended to "factors of production" other than land. (Harcourt 1972, p. 3)

In this chapter, I will attempt to reconstitute the epistemological trajectory that began with Ricardo's theory of differential rent and led to Sraffa's work and the Cambridge controversy.

Keynes and Sraffa's conceptions, along with those of the neo-Ricardian, are completely different from and incompatible with the neoclassical conception, as emphasized by the Cambridge controversy. These differences have implications for the construction of aggregate production functions (Felipe and McCombie 2005), the nature of macroeconomic equilibrium, the processes of convergence toward a steady-state position and, finally, the modalities of rent distribution (Bidard 2014).

A. Herscovici, *Essays on the Historicity of Capital*,
https://doi.org/10.1007/978-3-030-14838-6_5

For these reasons, the Keynesian and neo-Ricardian schools[1] emphasize the heterogeneous character of capital[2] and thus the logical impossibility (a) of conceiving an amount of aggregate capital as a constant value and (b) of deducing from the value of this capital the remuneration of factors of production.

According to Ricardo's theory, capital is conceived as a heterogeneous factor of production. For this purpose, I will begin my demonstration from Ricardo's original theory. This theory constitutes a *parable*: it provides the first elements of a theoretical construct in which capital is heterogeneous, thus announcing the Cambridge controversy.

Marshall's reading of the Ricardian theory is based on a homogeneous conception of capital. This interpretation sees in Ricardo the precursor of the neoclassical school: his theory of differential rent is conceived as a marginalist analysis in which marginal costs are increasing and in which the producer equals marginal cost and revenue; I will emphasize the limits of that interpretation.

In Part I, I will explain the basic mechanisms noted by Ricardo regarding the theory of differential rent. In Part II, I will compare Ricardo's analysis with Marshall's interpretation and show why the latter is incompatible with Ricardo's original analysis. In the third part, I will show how Sraffa extends Ricardo's analysis to the economy as a whole and to what extent this extension implies a refutation of the architecture of neoclassical macroeconomics.

1 Ricardo's Analysis: A First Approach

1.1 Ricardo's Model: Hypothesis and Overview

1.1.1 "Capital" Heterogeneity: A First Approach

The model is conceived based on an economy that produces a single good: corn. Added value is defined by the surplus of corn obtained at the end of the period considered based on the following reasons:

[1] Not only Sraffa but also Keynes had already begun to develop such an analysis. See Rotheim (1988).

[2] For this reason, in his growth model, Solow (1956) reasons from an economy that produces a single good.

first, advances[3] made by the capitalists are composed of wages and circulating capital. Second, at the end of the period, the revenue obtained allows the reconstitution of the circulating capital, the payment of wages, the receiving of an average profit and the eventual payment of the landowner's rent. All the variables are evaluated in corn quantities:

> On the land first cultivated, the return would be the same as before, namely, fifty per cent. or one hundred quarters of corn; but, the general profits of stock being regulated by the profits made on the least profitable employment of capital on agriculture, a division of the one hundred quarters would take place, forty-three per cent. or eighty-six quarters would constitute the profit of stock, and seven per cent. or fourteen quarters, would constitute rent. (Ricardo 1821, p. 53)

The production function can be represented as follows:

$$Y = \varphi\,[T, (l, c)] \tag{1}$$

where T represents the cultivated land; (l, c) represents the composite factor, namely, labor and circulating capital. Hypothetically, in an economy that produces a single good, l and c are obligatorily homogenous because they are evaluated in terms of the quantity of corn.

The problem of heterogeneity relates to the different qualities (i.e., different fertilities) of lands, which translates into different productivities. As Ricardo supposes, the fact that lands have different qualities means that T, *in Eq. (1) is heterogeneous.* T is composed of lands with different qualities (productivities): $t_1, t_2, \ldots, t_n$.

We observe here elements from which the works by Sraffa and the neo-Ricardian school developed (Robinson 1953–1954). The Cambridge controversy emphasizes the logical impossibility of measuring an aggregate amount of capital independent from the value of the distributive variables. This result is incompatible with the neoclassical theory of rent distribution: the remuneration of the factors of production is not determined from their respective contributions to the product (idem.).

---

[3] "Advances" is used in the sense employed by Quesnay.

From a logical point of view, it is impossible to calculate the marginal productivity of capital for the following reasons: the definition of marginal productivity (Kmp) of capital is as follows:

$$\text{Kmp} = \Delta Y/\Delta K \tag{2}$$

(Y is the total product and K, the total capital: Δ is related to variations).

This marginal productivity is equal to the interest rate, which is equal to the rate of profit (Garegnani 1980). When capital is a heterogeneous good, it must be expressed in value terms. This expression in value terms is a logical impossibility: to assess the marginal productivity of capital in value terms (and thus the rate of profit), it is necessary to know K and Y in value terms in advance; but to know K and Y in value terms, it is necessary to know in advance the rate of profit embedded in K and Y. In other words, to calculate the rate of profit, it is necessary to know this same rate of profit in advance. *Because one of the factors of production is heterogeneous, the concept of marginal productivity of this factor no longer makes sense.*

1.1.2 The Production Function Used by Ricardo

In light of these preliminary observations, I will interpret Ricardo's theory of differential rent based on the concept of decreasing returns to scale (Sraffa 1926, pp. 540 and 541):

Constant marginal productivity on land

t_1: $\Delta Yt_1/\Delta(l, c) =$ constant.

t_2: $\Delta Yt_2/\Delta(l, c) =$ constant.

Returns to scale are constant when we consider land homogeneity[4]:

$$\alpha Y_i = \varphi[\alpha\,(l, c), \alpha t_i] \tag{3}$$

with $\alpha > 0$.

[4]Kalecki (1990, p. 83) generalizes this hypothesis: he claims that in the industry, as the firm does not use its entire production capacity, marginal costs are constant.

While the land quality is constant, the returns of scale are constant. We reach the same conclusion as Bidard (2014, p. 5) when this author argues that "a slight change in external demand is made by a slight adaptation of activity levels with, on the physical side, no changes in the list of operated methods and cultivated lands and, on the value side, no change in prices and rents."

Returns to scale are decreasing when we consider land heterogeneity, i.e., different land qualities:

$$\alpha^{\beta} \cdot Y = \varphi[\alpha\,(l, c), \alpha\, t_i] \tag{4}$$

With $\alpha > 0$ and $1 > \beta > 0$.

Thus, the necessary and sufficient condition for the mechanism noted by Ricardo to occur is the existence of land heterogeneity; this mechanism operates fully without invoking the law of the diminishing marginal productivity of the factors of production. Such approach is confirmed by Ricardo in his *Principles*: "It is, then, because land is not unlimited in quantity and uniform in quality (…) that rent is ever paid for it" (Ricardo 1821, p. 41); land heterogeneity explains the increase of production costs and, consequently, decreasing returns. The "well-behaved" neoclassical Cobb-Douglass functions are characterized by constant returns to scale (Kaldor 1972); this constitutes a fundamental difference between the Ricardian analysis and the neoclassical analysis.

1.2 The Ricardian Model: The Main Mechanisms

1.2.1 The Ricardian Mechanism

Sraffa's analysis allows distinguishing two reasons to justify diminishing returns (1960, p. 238): diminishing returns are *extensive* when land is *heterogeneous*; returns are *intensive* when the quality of the land is constant; the increase of supply translates in the use of less productive methods of production (idem.). *These two situations are equivalent, since in both cases the increase in the unit value of the goods produced is due from the heterogeneous nature of land or capital.* Thus, the mechanisms highlighted by Ricardo and the neo-Ricardian school fully work when one of the factors of production is heterogeneous; such heterogeneity may be related to land or capital.

Change in the capital–labor ratio is an epiphenomenon, regarding the justification of diminishing returns: in this regard, Sraffa says that "(…) the essential is the change in the absolute size of the set of factors employees, then it is possible that their relationship does not vary" (Sraffa 1925, pp. 37, 53–54). Thus, for each dose of the composite factor applied to a land of the same quality, the unit production costs are constant (and not increasing, as Marshall guesses).

It is also important to draw a parallel with the analysis of Keynes in the General Theory. Keynes shows that there are different qualities of capital, each one with different marginal efficiencies; then in a second time, the marginal efficiency of total capital decreases with the total amount of capital used (see Chapter 6). This decrease in the marginal efficiency of capital means that, since the total quantity of capital increases, the system will make use of capital of "lower quality"; this mechanism acts as long as the marginal efficiency of capital is greater than the interest rate.

Such mechanism corresponds to the two problems studied by Sraffa: (a) the heterogeneity of capital, according to its different marginal efficiencies, and (b) the fact that such increase in production makes necessary to use capital of "worst" quality.

1.2.2 The Main Results

The following observations must be made regarding land rent:

1. Rent is not productive because it does not create value: *the rent is tied to the property, not to labor, the only source of value.*
2. Rent appears and its value increases due to the scarcity of land of better quality: *this scarcity turns the capital heterogeneous.*
3. The rent reflects a change in the modalities of distribution of the total value created by labor; it represents a cost that the capitalist must assume. Because value creation is entirely explained by direct and indirect amounts of labor, land itself does not create value.

According to Ricardo's theory, there are antagonisms among different social classes; more precisely, when wages rise, profits must decrease, and when land rent increases, profits also decrease. This result is completely incompatible with the Walrasian theory of *services producteurs*, according to which the remuneration of each factor is equal to its contribution to the product; this theory excludes, by definition, such distributive conflicts.

The marginal term does not refer to the ratio of the production factors (the capital–labor ratio in the standard neoclassical theory), but to the heterogeneity of the capital composed of different lands; from such a perspective, the marginal land is that which (a) determines the single price of corn, and (b) is not subject to private ownership because its production costs are so high that they would not allow the payment of rent to its owners (Schumpeter 1983, vol. II, pp. 397 and 398).

In neoclassical economics, the equalization of the rate of profits is explained by the fact that different firms have the same structure of costs and revenues, equal marginal costs and marginal products. For example, according to the theory of contestable markets (Baumol 1982), if a firm earns a profit π with a price above its marginal cost, performing a production y, this is an opportunity for *outsider* firms: such firms will enter the market offering a quantity $y + \xi$ and thus earn a profit of $\pi + \Delta\pi$. The competitive mechanism connected to the contestability of markets implies an increase in the amount produced, the disappearance of this rent and the return to the Pareto optimum. This auto-regulation mechanism acts when the amounts produced vary and when firms have the same cost structure.

In Ricardo's analysis, the equalization of the rate of profit is explained by the fact that capitalist firms have different cost structures (the rent to be paid is different, depending on the different land qualities), and average and marginal productivity are also different.[5] *The total production is exogenous; it cannot be conceived as an adjustment variable that allows the restoration of competitive conditions.*

[5]Sraffa (1960, pp. 238, 239) comes to this conclusion.

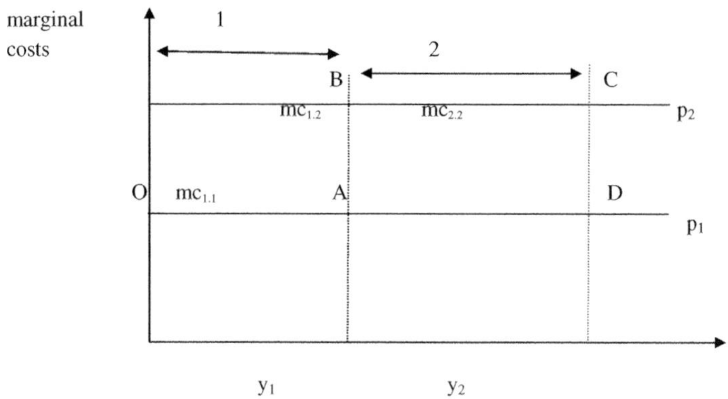

Fig. 1 Ricardo's model

As Ricardo states, price increases are determined by the conditions prevailing in lands of poorer quality. Consequently, the average cost obligatorily increases because lands with lower productivity are incorporated into the productive structure. The increase in the average cost is determined from the following mechanism: to the extent that by definition, $y_1 > y_2$ and $TC_1 = TC_2$, $AC_1 < AC_2$ (y_i represents land i production, TC_i the total cost and AC_i the average cost). This result is completely independent of the law of diminishing marginal productivity; this increase in the average total cost is explained by the heterogeneity of the land. The "physical" productivity of land 1 is constant for all times considered; during the first period, only land 1 is cultivated.

During the second period (BC segment on Fig. 1), lands t_1 and t_2 are cultivated; the productivity of t_2 is, by definition, lower than the productivity of t_1. During this second period, the productivity of t_1, measured in amount of corn per unit of capital, is constant. *The productivity differential is explained by the scarcity of better quality land*; scarcity explains (a) why inferior quality lands must be cultivated and consequently, (b) why there is a difference in costs. The rent appears (ABCD area) as a function of the average productivity differential between t_1 and t_2.

1.3 Capital Scarcity and Profit Rate

For Ricardo, population increase and the "development of society and wealth" (1821, p. 97) explain why it is necessary to cultivate lands of inferior quality; this translates into an increase in costs, which explains the appearance of land rent. Thus, the law of diminishing returns is explained based on an economic cause, not a physical one (Sraffa 1925, p 37); scarcity is by nature social and is caused by different social and economic developments, and by the initial rent distribution (Bidard 2014, p. 6).

Scarcity appears due to the *exogenous* increase of production. This scarcity explains, in turn, increasing costs and decreasing productivity. *Ricardo provides an economic definition of scarcity* (Gregory 1997, p 163.) *and an economic explanation of diminishing productivity*, "The characterization of the Ricardian theory, acknowledged by us as fundamental, i.e., assigns an economic cause *rather than a physical cause* to the diminishing productivity (...)" (Sraffa 1925, p. 37, emphasis added).

The neoclassical premises are always related to a "naturalist" approach, in regard to Economics: the analytical categories appear as universal. Marshall's interpretation of Ricardo illustrates perfectly such *démarche*: "(...) aspects within the classical scheme that were distorted by the vulgar economists, who turned economics into a taxonomic identification of unchanging natural laws in a world inevitably characterized by scarcity (...)" (Martins 2013, p. 14).

In Ricardo's scheme, the logical sequence can be stated as follows: an *exogenous change in rent distribution* is translated into a change in the demand for corn. This increase in demand corresponds to land "heterogenization," by increased costs and the need to exploit lands of inferior quality. Finally, this process is translated into a new change in rent distribution: the relative share of rent and wages increases, whereas the relative share of profit diminishes. Ricardo's analysis is dynamic as it "consists in following the transformation of a long-term equilibrium when demand increases" (Bidard 2014, p. 3); such transformation includes the modification of the equilibrium values.

Table 1 Scarcity, production costs and distribution

Neoclassical economics: physical scarcity → prices of production factors → rent distribution. Variations in production allow the maintenance of conditions for profit maximization. ***Scarcity is physical: it is the key variable***
Ricardian economics: economic development → initial rent distribution → scarcity → change in rent distribution. Variations in production are exogenous and do not constitute an adjustment variable for the position that corresponds to the maximization of profit. ***Scarcity is social: it is the variable determined***

At this point, the assumptions of the neo-Ricardian analysis appear: there is an exogenous determination of distributive variables, and this exogenous determination constitutes the cause of scarcity and of increase in average costs; the value of a certain aggregate amount of capital cannot be measured independently of the value of distributive variables.

In neoclassical economics, the rent distribution is determined by the "physical" scarcity of the production factors; and the economic growth is limited by this "natural" scarcity. In Ricardian economics, causality is different: the general development level of the society and the initial rent distribution determine the scarcity, which determines the changes in rent distribution; the increase of the land rent allows explaining why the system tends to converge toward a stationary state (Table 1).

We can establish a parallel with Keynes's General Theory: Keynes defines scarcity as the reason why the return of capital is higher than its costs and the interest rate. However, Keynes differentiates quantities and economic values; when investment increases, the marginal efficiency of capital decreases, but Keynes notes that this decrease in the marginal efficiency of capital does not mean that capital is less productive *in physical terms* (GT, p. 169).

The neo-Ricardian and Keynesian approaches, on one hand, and the neoclassical one on the other hand, have different ontological conceptions of the nature of capital. The former approaches define capital from its social and "expectational" dimensions, i.e., in its historical dimension: (a) its value depends on variables related to the rent distribution and/or to the expectations, (b) the concept of scarcity is not defined from the relative quantities of factors (Pasinetti 1997), and (c) the rent distribution is not deduced from such scarcity. There is a feedback effect between the rent distribution and the scarcity: first, the rent distribution determines the scarcity, and then scarcity modifies the initial rent distribution.

In neoclassical economics, price is determined based on the interaction of supply and demand; the construction of the supply function implies the adoption of the law of diminishing marginal productivity, and such law is conceived in physical terms: only increasing marginal costs allow the construction of a well-behaved supply function and thus explain the price based on the interaction of supply and demand (Sraffa 1925, p. 46); such construction is closely related to the utility theory of value. If this law of diminishing marginal productivity is not verified, then the interplay of supply and demand no longer explains the formation of prices (idem., p. 21).

In this case, the labor theory of value provides an alternative explanation that is based on direct and indirect labor costs. The classical economists, from Smith to Ricardo and Marx, showed that the interplay of supply and demand determines only temporary deviations between market prices and natural prices and that the former converge into the value of the latter. The determination of these natural prices (or in Marx's terminology, prices of production) is explained from the labor theory of value.

2 Ricardo and Marshall: Two Incompatible Interpretations

2.1 Marshall's Analysis

2.1.1 The "Land Switching"

With respect to Ricardo's theory of differential rent, Marshall states, "(...) Our law establishes that sooner or later (...) a point will be reached after which all additional doses [of the composite factor] will obtain a lower yield in proportion to the preceding doses" (Marshall 1920, p. 145).

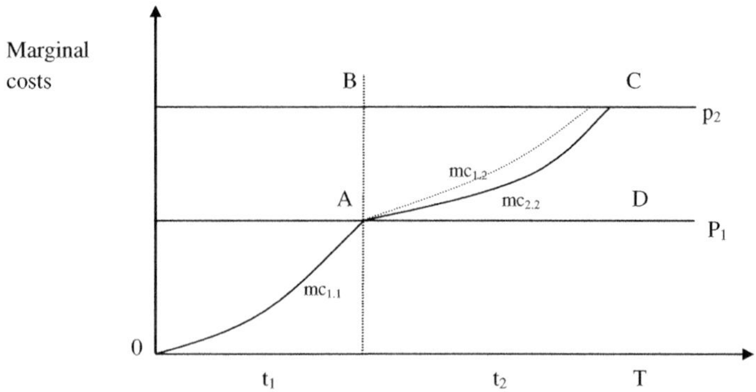

Fig. 2 The Marshallian analysis and the "exchange" of lands

This interpretation allows the statement that the extensive conception obligatorily originated from the intensive concept (Jessua 1991, p. 188): *in a land of equal quality*, the increase in the composite factor corresponds to a decrease in the supplementary product. *The application of a supplementary dose, beyond a certain value, would result in a deficit of exploitation with a marginal cost higher than the marginal revenue* ($mc_{1.2}$ *in Fig. 2); the fact of cultivating inferior quality lands allows one, momentarily, to keep the marginal cost at such a level that capitalist exploitation will generate a profit.*

The point at which an (increasing) marginal cost becomes equal to the marginal product is defined based on a critical value of the ratio C/t_i. For this reason, the Marshallian concept used in neoclassical theory is intensive.

$mc_{1.1}$ represents the marginal cost of land 1 during period 1, and $mc_{1.2}$ represents the marginal cost of land of quality 1 in period 2, as the ratio C/t_i increases, *in the same land*, in the second period. This does not occur because the capitalists exploit lands of inferior quality in this second period. Rather, *this mechanism implies that there is an update of the costs and unit prices depending on the different periods considered*: the cost of the production realized on land 1 in the second period is equal to $mc_{1.1} + R_{1.2}$, which is equal to $mc_{2.2}$. The curve of the capital marginal cost is represented by the solid line curve $mc_{1.1}$ and $mc_{2.2}$.

From West (1815) to Marshall (1920) and Blaug (1992), we find the following arguments:

(a) Capitalists stop investing on land of a given quality when an increase in the *C*/*T* ratio makes their marginal costs higher than the marginal productivity obtained from the land. That is why they exploit a land of inferior quality: there, *the lowest yield of T will be compensated by the fact that the marginal cost is lower than the marginal productivity of C; this mechanism allows the momentary restoration of the rate of profit in the land of inferior quality:* (Wetz, op. cit., p. 14): in period 2, $c_2/t_2 < c_1/t_1$, which implies $mc_{2.2} < mc_{1.2}$ (see Fig. 2).
(b) *Diminishing marginal productivity implies that average productivity is also diminishing* (Blaug 1992, p. 90). On lands with quality t_1, c/t_1 increases until the marginal cost is equal to the price (or marginal product); on land t_2, the amounts of capital will gradually increase until c_2/t_2 equals the price. Because the average productivity in t_2 is obligatorily lower than the average productivity in t_1, as Marshall states, the theory of differential rent is explained based on the law of diminishing marginal productivity; Marshall states, with respect to the rent generated by adding a dose of labor and capital, that "(…) it does not matter if it is applied to a poor or to a rich land; it is sufficient that it is the last dose that can be applied profitably to this land" (op. cit., p. 146).

2.1.2 Marshall Versus Ricardo

The Marshallian interpretation obligatorily verifies the following relationships:

$$\mathrm{mc}_1 = \varphi_1(c_1/t_1), \text{ with } \varphi_1' > 0 \tag{5}$$

$$\mathrm{mp}_1 = \varphi_2\,(c_1/t_1), \text{ with } \varphi_2' < 0 \tag{6}$$

$$\mathrm{mc}_2 = \varphi_3\,(c_2/t_2), \text{ with } \varphi_3' > 0 \tag{7}$$

$$\text{mp}_2 = \varphi_4(c_2/t_2), \text{ with } \varphi_4' < 0 \tag{8}$$

(mc_i is the marginal cost in land i and mp_1 is the marginal productivity of i).

The observation of Fig. 2 shows that at the beginning of the first period, c_1/t_1 increases until the marginal cost is equal to p_1. The "*land exchange*" occurs at this point. Capitalists apply increasing amounts of the composite factor on land 2 until $\text{mc}_{2.2} = p_2$. I will call the equilibrium point the situation in which on a land of given quality, the marginal cost of the composite factor equals its marginal productivity. The equilibriums of two periods correspond to the following situation:

Period1

$$\text{mc}_{1.1} = p_1 \tag{9}$$

Period 2

$$\text{mc}_{1.1} + R_{1.2} = p_2 = \text{mc}_{2.2} \tag{10}$$

($R_{1.2}$ is the rent that the capitalist must pay for land 1 at period 2).

Proposition 1 The factors of production are considered fully substitutable; this allows for building "well-behaved" macroeconomic production functions and implementing mechanisms of convergence toward a steady-state position in the models of economic growth (Dvoskin and Saverio 2016).

The Marshallian interpretation is contradictory. The validation of the law of diminishing marginal productivity, or of increasing marginal cost, for a heterogeneous set implies the following modification of Eqs. (5)–(8):

$$\text{mc} = \varphi_5(C/t_1 + t_2) = \varphi_5(C/T) \tag{11}$$

With $\varphi_5' > 0$

$$\text{mp} = \varphi_6(C/t_1 + t_2) = \varphi_6(C/T) \tag{12}$$

With $\varphi_6' > 0$.

In this case, if T is heterogeneous, the law of increasing marginal costs is not tested, in a continuous way, for each type of land.

Proposition 2 Based on Eq. (10), it is possible to deduce that at equilibrium:

$$mc_{1.1} < mc_{2.2} \tag{13}$$

If, as assumed by the neoclassical analysis, returns to scale are constant, relationship (13) obligatorily implies that *this difference is explained by a difference of capital intensity on both types of land.* In Fig. 2, A represents the first point of land exchange: at A, there is profit maximization; between B and C, $mc_{1.2} > mc_{2.2}$, the capitalist exploiting land 2 will increase the amount of the composite factor until arriving at C. Because the price of corn is determined by the worst conditions of production, to the right of A, the price increases from p_1 to p_2; the AB portion represents the additional cost that the capitalist on land 1 must pay to the rent owner.

There is a fundamental ambiguity: the marginal costs increase for two reasons, not only because the C/T ratio increases in a land of equal quality but also because it is necessary to exploit lands of poorer quality. It is the increase in production that generates (a) an increase in the price of corn, (b) an increase in the average cost and (c) an increase in the costs of scarce lands in the form of differential rent. As emphasized by Sraffa (1925, p. 24), there is no way to differentiate the impact of these two effects on average productivity. On the other hand, *it is impossible to think in terms of marginal cost when one of the factors of production (T) is not homogeneous.* Finally, while the different lands are not exhausted (before A and C), the capitalists act as a monopoly, with the price above the marginal cost (Sraffa 1926).

Marshall's reading is inconsistent with Ricardo's theory, which argues as follows:

(i) *There is an update of the marginal cost for land 1*, depending on the period considered. In the second period, the cost to exploit better quality lands is $mc_{1.1} + R_{1.2}$ (Eq. 10); this difference is explained based on the rent that the capitalist must pay, $R_{1.2}$. In this sense, I agree with Marcuzzo and Rosselli's criticism (2011): the marginal characteristics are extended to the whole stock, and it is not possible to consider the *ceteris paribus* condition.

(ii) The land is not a homogeneous factor of production; *the substitution of factors of production is, by nature, limited*; consequently, we can thus consider that the coefficients of production are fixed (Dockès 1971). Equations (5)–(8) are not verified for lands of different quality. *It is impossible to reconcile, as Marshall does, land heterogeneity and the law of diminishing marginal productivity (or the law of increasing marginal costs): land heterogeneity limits the substitutability of the factors of production*, and this substitutability cannot be applied to a heterogeneous set of lands.

It is possible to draw a parallel with the *reswitching* of techniques; if we consider that land heterogeneity is equivalent to heterogeneity of the production methods used (Sraffa 1960, p. 238), we find the same type of limitations as those highlighted by the Cambridge controversy: the monotonic relationship between C/T ratio (the capital/labor ratio in the controversy) and the marginal productivity (the interest rate in the controversy) is not verified for any value of C/T.

The Marshallian analysis is explained based on an *intensive* conception because the marginal productivity of the factors depends only on the C/T ratio, regardless of the production scale. This production scale has no influence on the average returns because the returns to scale are constant. For this law to be applicable, the factors of production must be fully substitutable and therefore homogeneous. It is the reason why Schumpeter states that theorists assimilating Ricardo's theory of differential rent into the theory of marginal productivity of factors of production "(…) do not generalize Ricardo's scheme but instead destroy it" (Schumpeter 1983, p. 739) (Fig. 3).

Ricardo's analysis includes an *extensive* concept of marginal cost and marginal productivity; likewise, in Keynes's economics, what matters is capital heterogeneity, not the C/T ratio (Pasinetti 1997). As Sraffa states, the "law" of diminishing marginal productivity is primarily explained by the "increasing size of the branch of activity (…)" (1925, p. 24), not by modifying the proportion of the quantities of the two factors. In this regard, he states, "(…) the increase in the size of the branch of activity could also be the result of an increase of all factors of production" (idem.).

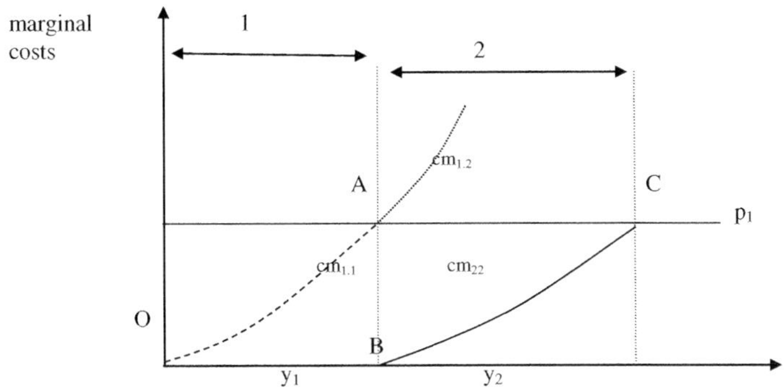

Fig. 3 The Marshall's hypothesis

2.2 Marshall's These: The Equivalency Between Quantities and Values

Equivalency between values and quantities is the fundamental assumption that allows to constructs neoclassical production functions and thus determines the main relationships of neoclassical macroeconomics. The scarcity of production factors is assessed by physical quantities: in the Cobb-Douglas function, which is written in the form $Y = f(K, L)$, K represents the capital quantity and L the labor quantity.

Marshall's contradiction may be expressed in the following terms: on one hand, equivalence between values and quantities constitutes the foundations of the neoclassical analysis; such equivalence is only possible when returns of scale are constant. On the other hand, returns of scale constant imply in land homogeneity. *It is not possible to verify simultaneously the equivalence between values and quantities and the heterogeneity of the land; in other words, the heterogeneity of the land (and by extension of the capital) does not allow deducing such equivalence; the Cambridge controversy will develop this analysis.*

If AC_{ij} represents the average cost of corn obtained on land i in period j,

$c_1 + c_2/y_1 + y_2$ is equal to c_1/y_1.

$$AC_{1.1} = AC_{1.2} = AC_{2.2} \tag{14}$$

where c_i *is the quantity of composite factor used during period i,* y_i is the corn produced on land of quality and AC_{ij} is the corn average cost on the land *i* during period *j*.

Equation (14) is expressed in terms of "physical" quantities, i.e., say in corn quantities.

The average cost on land 1, evaluated in quantity of corn, is the same in both periods; 'physical' productivity is constant on all periods considered. The law of constant returns to scale implies that the unitary value of corn, evaluated from labor quantity, during the two periods considered, is equal to p_i. The average value is constant over the two periods considered:

$$p_i \mathrm{AC}_{1.1} = p_i \mathrm{AC}_{1.2} = p_i \mathrm{AC}_{2.2} \tag{15}$$

Equations (14) and (15) allow to assert that, when costs evaluated in physical units are constant, they are also constant in value; it is possible to note *an equivalence and a proportional relationship between physical quantities and values*, which corresponds to the Marshallian hypothesis used by neoclassical economics. This is a manifestation of the money neutrality: value expressed in monetary unities is the simple reflection of the real economy evaluated in physical quantities.

When, on the contrary, returns of scale are decreasing, the unitary value of corn, measured by the quantity of labor, increases with the exploitation of poorer quality land: p_1 is necessarily less than p_2. The equation in physical units (that is to say in quantities) can be written as follows:

$$\mathrm{AC}_{1.1} = \mathrm{AC}_{1.2} < \mathrm{AC}_{2.2} \tag{16}$$

because physical productivity of land 1 is constant. The equation in value changes as follows:

$$p_1 \cdot \mathrm{AC}_{1.1} < p_2 \left(\mathrm{AC}_{1.2} + R_{1.2}\right) = p_2 \cdot \mathrm{AC}_{2.2} \tag{17}$$

($R_{1.2}$ is the land rent that the capitalist who cultivates the best land has to pay the landowner during the period 2).

In the Ricardian system, this equivalence between quantities and values is not checked when the land is heterogeneous. The quantity of corn produced on the land 1 is the same in both periods. Nevertheless, these same quantities, measured in value, are different depending on the period considered, and this for the following reason: *the value of the average cost of land 1 is updated during the period 2.* This updating mechanism is performed based (a) on the increase of corn value and (b) on the payment of land rent which adds to production costs. Comparing (16) and (17) shows that there is no equivalence between quantities and values:

> It is true that, on the best land, the same produce will still be obtained with the same labor as before, but its value would be enhanced in consequence of the diminished returns obtained by those who employed fresh labor and stock on the less fertile land. (Ricardo 1821, p. 44)

The hypothesis of constant return to scale is necessary to prove the equivalence between quantities and values; nevertheless, it is incompatible with the Ricardian rent, because such rent comes from the land productivity differential, i.e., land heterogeneity.

Ricardo's analysis is performed at the aggregate level (C/T or C/Y), returns are constant at the microeconomic level, and decreasing at the aggregate level; it highlights why land heterogeneity explains the modification of corn value over different periods. Marshall's analysis is essentially microeconomic (c_i/t_i), returns are decreasing at the microeconomic level and constant at the aggregate level. Marshall postulates homogeneity of production factor, which implies that the value of corn is constant. The Marshallian "reductionism" is expressed by the primacy of the microeconomic analysis, that is to say, by the fact of reducing the overall macroeconomic mechanisms to their microeconomic foundations: in this sense, Marshall's contribution is essential to design the neoclassical standard macroeconomics.

There is an extension of these parables to other forms of capital: the neoclassical school, from Marshall's work, conceives capital as homogeneous, allows it, among other things, to justify the Cobb-Douglas production functions, and to explain the distribution of revenues from the scarcity of factors of production as measured by the capital/labor ratio, the latter being assessed by quantities. The neo-Ricardian school highlights the heterogeneity of capital, which leads to a refutation of all the neoclassical macroeconomic relationships, from a different concept of scarcity.

3 Sraffa and the Criticism of Marshall's Interpretation

3.1 The Land Heterogeneity Parable

In his book, "Production of Commodities by Means of Commodities," Sraffa (1960, p. 37 and following) explicitly refutes the Marshallian interpretation. He compares two situations: the first is characterized by the heterogeneity of lands, and the second is characterized by their homogeneity.

In the first case, the approach is *extensive* (idem., p. 238) because the quality of the lands becomes "worse" due to increased production, i.e., there is a scarcity of better quality land. *Sraffa considers that the situation in which the land is heterogeneous and the methods of production are homogeneous is equivalent to the situation in which the land is homogeneous and the methods of production are heterogeneous* (ibid., p. 237). Thus, in the second case, various production methods are used simultaneously; to increase production, increasingly less productive methods will be required. There will thus be a difference in productivity between the different methods used.[6]

For a particular method of production, the land has a limited production capacity: beyond this capacity, production methods allow the production of a greater quantity of corn but represent a higher unit cost (ibid., p. 238). Because it is not possible to meet the increase in demand by exploiting lands of superior quality, it is necessary to resort to more "expensive" production methods; the rent appears in the land cultivated with the "cheaper" method.

This analysis can be applied to industrial production: excess in demand relative to supply creates a scarcity of certain goods. Their prices increase, which allows their production using either methods that are more expensive or methods that incorporate a larger amount of

[6]This is the same case studied by Keynes (GT, p. 119).

labor.[7] If the total production uses, for example, two production methods m_1 and m_2, with m_1 being that which corresponds to the smaller amount of labor per unit, and the price is determined based on m_2, there will be a differential in costs and rates of profit in that industry: firms that use m_1 will appropriate a quasi-rent, whereas those using m_2 will earn a lower rate of profit. Such a situation is incompatible with a situation of pure and perfect competition for the following reasons:

(a) Due to the fact that there is no equalization of rates of profit, firms that use m_1 benefit from a monopoly rent because they do not equate their marginal costs with price.
(b) There is no mechanism linked to a component of supply that will make this rent disappear in the long run.
(c) The only factor that explains the existence and permanence of rents is scarcity, which is caused by an increase in social demand (ibid., p. 239). Thus, the two situations analyzed—land heterogeneity and homogeneity of production methods or land homogeneity and heterogeneity of production methods—are equivalent (Grégory 1997, p. 160).

3.2 The Theoretical Implications

Proposition 1 Heterogeneity is manifested with respect to different qualities of land or to different production methods of production for the same land quality. In both cases, the situation is incompatible with the results of neoclassical economics: (a) Land heterogeneity does not allow for conceiving an aggregate amount of capital independently from the value of distributive variables and (b) The heterogeneity of production methods does not allow for verifying the results of pure and perfect Walrasian competition, that is, the law of increasing marginal costs and the equalization of marginal costs with marginal product.

[7]The parallel with the analysis made by Keynes in his GT is obvious; in this regard, see Pasinetti (1997). In the Keynesian analysis, various qualities of capital operate during the same period.

These two modes of heterogenization allow the establishment of a parallel between Sraffa and Keynes. For Keynes, an exogenous decrease in the interest rate makes capitals that were previously unprofitable to become profitable (Pasinetti 1997; Rotheim 1988). *This implies that there is heterogeneity of production methods; consequently, capital cannot be conceived as a homogeneous factor* at the aggregate level, and the rule of equalization of marginal cost and revenue is not verified.

Proposition 2 In both cases studied, we are in the presence of *decreasing returns to scale*; this characteristic is inconsistent with an aggregate production function of the Cobb-Douglas type, which is a new refutation of the aggregate production functions.

Proposition 3 This heterogenization corresponds to an update of the capital value in each period: as the value of corn increases, capital value also increases. Thus, contrary to the neoclassical analysis, it is not possible to consider that the value of an aggregate amount of capital can be constant and determined independently from the distributive variables.

Proposition 4 *The Marshallian concept of increasing marginal costs only applies to the intra-marginal level*, i.e., for lands of the same quality. The *tour de force* consists of extending this mechanism to the inter-marginal level, i.e., to lands of different quality. *In Ricardian economics, on the contrary, intra-marginal costs are constant and inter-marginal costs are increasing*, which proves that the latter do not depend on the former.

Proposition 5 Finally, it is possible to state that the neoclassical construct focuses on an analysis of the different components of supply and the mechanisms of self-regulation attached to them. In contrast, the distributive variables and the modifications resulting from demand play an active role in Sraffian analysis because these are the variables that cause scarcity.

Final Remarks

It is not possible to interpret Ricardo's theory of differential rent as the assumptions of the marginalist school and its fundamentals, i.e., the law of diminishing marginal productivity, the equalization between marginal cost and marginal revenue, and the determination of price based on the law of supply and demand. The interpretation provided by Sraffa shows that (a) the theory of differential rent can be explained without resorting to these laws and that (b) the results thus obtained are totally incompatible with the fundamentals of Marshallian economics.

It is also important to highlight the methodological convergences between Ricardo's method and results and those employed by Keynes in his General Theory. For Ricardo, Sraffa and Keynes, social scarcity explains profit and rent: (a) with respect to Sraffa's analysis, I showed that firms using the most efficient methods of production benefit from quasi-rent; and (b) for Keynes, an increase in investment during the same period causes various *vintages* of capital to coexist with differentiated returns (GT p. 119). This mechanism is intrinsically linked to capital heterogeneity and the production methods used.

Finally, an aggregate amount of capital cannot be conceived using a value that is constant and independent from distributive or "expectational" variables. For the neo-Ricardian school, this is the subject of the Cambridge controversy; with respect to Keynes, a modification of long-term expectations is obligatorily translated into a modification of the value of this amount of aggregate capital.[8]

[8]Such mechanism will be demonstrated in the next chapter.

References

Baumol, W.J. 1982. Contestable Markets: An Uprising in the Theory of Industry Structure. *American Economic Review* 72 (1): 1–15.
Bidard, Christian. 2014. *The Ricardian Rent Theory Two Centuries After.* Document de travail Working Paper 2014-54, Université de Paris Ouest Nanterre la Défense.
Blaug, Mark. 1992. *The Methodology of Economics or How Economists Explain*, 2nd ed. Cambridge: Cambridge University Press.
Dockès, Pierre. 1971. Introduction. In *Des principes de l'économie politique et de l'impôt*, ed. Ricardo David. Paris: Flammarion.
Dvoskin, Ariel, and Saverio M. Fratini. 2016. On the Samuelson-Etula Master Function and the Capital Controversy. *The European Journal of the History of Economic Thought* 23 (6): 1032–1058. https://doi.org/10.1080/09672567.2016.1186920.
Felipe, Jesus, and J.S.L. McCombie. 2005. How Sound Are the Foundations of the Aggregate Production Function? *Eastern Economic Journal* 31 (3) (Summer): 467–488.
Garegnani, Pierangelo. 1980. Sobre a teoria da distribuição e do valor em Marx e nos economistas clássicos. *Progresso técnico e teoria econômica.* São Paulo: Hucitec-Unicamp.
Gregory, Christopher A. 1997. Political Economy, Household Economy and the Price of Land: Towards a Decolonization of Social Sciences Imperialism. In *Capital Controversy, Post-Keynesian Economics and the History of Economic Thought: Essays in Honour of Geoff Harcourt Volume One*, ed. Philip Arestis, Gabriel Palma, and Malcolm Sawyer. London and New York: Routledge.
Harcourt, G.C. 1972. *Some Cambridge Controversies in the Theory of Capital.* Cambridge: Cambridge University Press.
Jessua, Claude. 1991. *Histoire de la théorie économique.* Paris: Presses Universitaires de France.
Kaldor, Nicholas. 1972. The Irrelevance of Equilibrium Economics. *Economic Journal, Royal Economic Society* 82 (328) (December): 1237–1255. Handle: RePEc:ecj:econjl:v:8.
Kalecki, Michal. 1990 [1939]. *Crescimento e ciclo das economias capitalistas.* São Paulo: Hucitec.
Keynes, John Maynard. 2009 [1936]. *The General Theory of Employment, Interest and Money.* New York: Classic Books America.
Marcuzzo, Maria Cristina, and Rosselli Annalisa. 2011. Sraffa and His Arguments Against 'Marginism'. *Cambridge Journal of Economics* 35: 219–231.

Marshall, Alfred. 1920. *Principles of Economics*, 8th ed. London: Macmillan.
Martins, Nuno Ornela. 2013. *The Cambridge Contribution to the Revival of Classical Political Economy*. London and New York: Routledge.
Pasinetti, Luigi L. 1997. The Marginal Efficiency of Investment. *A "Second Edition" of the General Theory—Vol. 1*, ed. G.C. Harcourt and P.A. Riach, 198–218. London and New York: Routledge.
Ricardo, David. 1821. *On the Principles of Political Economy and Taxation*, 3rd ed. Ontario: Batoche Book 2001.
Robinson, Joan. 1953–1954. The Production Function and the Theory of Capital. *Review of Economic Studies* xxi: 81–106.
Rotheim, Roy J. 1988. Keynes and the Marginalist Theory of Distribution. *Journal of Post Keynesian Economics* 20 (3) (Spring): 355–387.
Schumpeter, Joseph A. 1983 [1954]. *Histoire de l'analyse économique. L'âge classique—II*. Paris: Gallimard.
Solow, Robert. 1956. A Contribution to the Theory of Economic Growth. *Quarterly Journal of Economics* 70: 65–94.
Sraffa, Piero. 1925. Sulle relazioni fracosto e quantitá prodotta. *Annali di Ecónomia* II (1): 277–328.
———. 1926. The Laws of Returns Under Competitive Conditions. *The Economic Journal* 36 (144) (December): 535–550.
———. 1972 [1960]. *Produção de Mercadorias por Meio de Mercadorias. Prelúdio para uma Crítica da Teoria Econômica*. Rio de Janeiro: Zahar Editores.
West, Edward. 1815. *The Application of Capital to Land*, ed. Jacob H. Hollander. Baltimore: The Johns Hopkins Press.

6

The Nature of Capital in the General Theory: Theoretical Implications and Structural Instability

> Keynes (…) was extremely skeptical of the traditional view that one could identify something called a quantity of capital independent of values. Surely, under the influence of Sraffa (….), Keynes went so far as to rule out the logical possibility of the phrase marginal productivity of capital. (Rotheim 1998)

This chapter aims to develop the methodological and epistemological implications of Pasinetti (1997) and Rotheim's (1998) works with regard to Keynes' conception of the nature of capital, as expressed in the General Theory (GT).

Such conception is contradictory to the neoclassical framework: Keynes refutes the neoclassical theory of distribution by refuting the second postulate of the "classical" theory and the loanable funds theory (GT, Chapter XIV). He demonstrates why the determination of the interest rate must be exogenous and not determined by "real" variables. It is possible to affirm that Keynes refutes the existence of a labor market and of a capital market the way they are defined by the neoclassical school.[1] Anticipating the Cambridge Controversy, Keynes shows why an aggregate quantity of capital cannot be conceived as constant over time.

[1]With regard to the first point, see Barrère (1985, p. 43), and for the second, see Petri (1998).

A. Herscovici, *Essays on the Historicity of Capital*,
https://doi.org/10.1007/978-3-030-14838-6_6

Finally, it is possible to demonstrate why such conception of capital implies structural instability of the system as defined by Vercelli (1985). The modalities of aggregation of heterogeneous capitals used by Keynes provide the elements to construct an endogenous analysis of the cycle, and to explain the switching between expansion and recession. I will demonstrate how the specific concept of scarcity (or abundance) of capital used by Keynes, as well as the modification of long-run expectations, explains the cyclical movement.

In the first section, I will study the modalities used by Keynes to construct the aggregate Investment function. For such purposes, I will define the investment function and its components and I will analyze the determinants of interest rate, as well as the role and determinants of the long-run expectations. I will explicate the method used by Keynes to aggregate different vintages of capital. In the second section, I will explicate the implications linked to this conception of capital, and will highlight the similarities between this approach and the classical one (mainly that by Smith, Ricardo and Marx). Then I will demonstrate why there is no stability of the aggregate equilibrium, and how it is possible to build simple mechanisms that produce endogenous fluctuations. In relation to this aspect, I will highlight the convergences and the complementarities between Keynes' and the neo-Ricardian approach.

1 The Aggregate Investment Function

1.1 The Different Components

1.1.1 The Marginal Efficiency of Capital

Keynes initially defines three concepts: *Z*, the aggregate supply price function; *D*, the aggregate demand function; and *e*, the marginal efficiency of capital.

The supply price of capital asset is "(….) the price which would just induce a manufacturer newly to produce an additional unit of such assets. i.e., what is sometimes called its replacement cost" (GT, p. 112)

(*Proposition 1*). The demand price is "(...) the proceeds which entrepreneurs expect to receive from the employment of N men (...)" (GT, p. 23).

The marginal efficiency of capital is defined as "(....) that rate of discount which would make the present value of the series of annuities given by the return expected from the capital-asset during its life just equal to its supply price" (GT, p. 112) (*Proposition 2*). Finally, the supply price is related to the current value of capital, and not to the value at which it was bought by the entrepreneur (*Proposition 3*).

From proposition 1, it is possible to deduce that the supply price corresponds to the maximization of the expected profit of the entrepreneur who produces such assets. From propositions 2 and 3, we can deduce that there is an *update* of capital asset, in regard to the period considered; *such update is relative to the value of capital asset and to its prospective yields.*

From proposition 2, we can write:

$$P_o = \frac{\sum_1^n \mathrm{Qi}}{(1+e)^n} \qquad (1)$$

$(\Sigma \mathrm{Qi}/(1 + e)^{n})$ represents the updated value of the prospective yield during its life, with P_o being the supply price, ΣQi the long-term expected proceeds and e the marginal efficiency of the capital.

From (1), we can deduce that the marginal efficiency of capital depends on two variables: the long-run expectations of the prospective yield on capital assets and the supply price of those capital assets. *The higher the long-run expectations, the higher the marginal efficiency of capital, for P_o constant; the higher the supply price, the lower the marginal efficiency, for* ΣQi *constant.*

The demand price of investment is the current value of a financial asset updated to the current interest rate (GT, p. 113):

$$P_\mathrm{d} = \frac{\sum_1^n \mathrm{Ri}}{(1+r)^n} \qquad (2)$$

$(\Sigma \mathrm{Ri}/(1 + r)^{n})$ represents the updated value of the prospective yield, r the interest rate, and P_d the demand price (GT, p. 113).

Keynes' theory is based upon a choice of assets mechanism (Carvalho 1992, p. 168). Individuals choose assets: money, financial or productive assets. From such a perspective, the entrepreneur's choice will be made between the money, the prospective yield of the investment and the prospective yield of a financial asset.

With regard to the supply price, Eq. (1) may be interpreted as the equalization between the marginal cost of capital and the marginal product. However, such interpretation is erroneous: Keynes' mechanism is based upon *expected* and not effective yield. From the strong uncertainty which characterizes the Keynesian universe, it is not possible to equalize marginal costs and effective marginal product, but only marginal costs and expected marginal value product; concretely, it is impossible to maximize a microeconomic function of profit.

1.1.2 The Investment Function

The investment decision may be explained by the comparison between the marginal efficiency of capital and interest rate: if the marginal efficiency of capital is superior to the interest rate, entrepreneurs will invest in productive capital. They will compare the expected profitability of the investment and the profitability of o financial asset, and will choose the former.

For certain authors (Robinson 1983, p. 331), the difference between marginal efficiency of capital and interest rate must be positive. This difference represents a risk premium to compensate the risk investment in productive capital.[2] Such concept is also developed by Barrère (1985, p. 82), and it corresponds to the monetary incitation necessary to "decide the entrepreneurs to assume the risks of the production."

Keynes initially considers that *each kind of capital* is characterized by a negative correlation between the investment level and the marginal efficiency of capital (GT, p. 113): the marginal efficiency of capital decreases when the investment increases.

[2] We may observe that the yields of the productive asset are uncertain, while the yields of a financial asset, as a bond, are certain, by the determination of the interest rate applied (Dow 1985, p. 159).

In the *short run*, new investments are realized when $P_o < P_d$, i.e., when the marginal efficiency of capital is higher than the interest rate: "The marginal efficiency of investment is favorable if it is high relative to other returns, particularly the rate of interest on bonds" (Dow 1985, p. 159). The increase of the demand for capital implies that the supply price increases. When ΣQi is constant, in the short run (Eq. (1)), the marginal efficiency of capital must decrease; the adjustment toward the equilibrium is realized by the price variation (Davidson 1978, p. 70).

In the long run, expectations will change: the output of investment realized today" will have to compete (....) with the output from equipment produced subsequently (....). Moreover, entrepreneur's profit (...) will be reduced, if all output comes to be produced cheaply" (GT, p. 117). *In the long run*, "the prospective yield will fall as the supply of that type of capital is increased (....)" (idem.). From Eq. (1), we can deduce that a decrease in ΣQi corresponds to a decrease in *e*, when P_o is constant.

We can capture such mechanism from the concepts of stock and flow equilibrium (Asimakopulos 1991, pp. 104 and 105). The former concerns long-term equilibrium and the latter, short-term equilibrium.[3] Each asset depends on three attributes: *q*, the expected yield, *c* the carrying cost and *l* the liquidity premium (TG, p. 191). If *a* is the expected appreciation of the asset in terms of itself, the return of each asset is equal to $(q - c + l + a)$. If we consider, for example, two productive assets and the money, and if we suppose the carrying costs negligible, the stock equilibrium implies that the return of each asset is equal:

$$q_1 + a_1 = q_2 + a_2 = l_3 \qquad (3)$$

(*qi* as the expected return of the investment and *a* as its supply price). Assets 1 and 2 are productive assets and asset 3 is the money.

The flow equilibrium is realized when the expected return of investment is the same as the one of a financial asset, i.e., when:

$$P_o = P_d \qquad (4)$$

[3]Such mechanism is analyzed by Davidson, from the concept of short-period flow-supply price of capital (1978, pp. 70 and 71).

Let us suppose an initial situation with a stock equilibrium and, for example, a decrease in interest rate: P_o becomes inferior to P_d, and such situation corresponds to the realization of productive investment. P_o will increase until $P_o = P_d$: but such increase does not allow verifying the stock equilibrium, as a_1 and a_2 increase. The restoration of the stock equilibrium implies that q_1 e q_2 decrease, i.e., that *long-term expectations decrease*. When such equilibrium is reached, decrease in q_1 and q_2 does not verify the conditions of flow equilibrium any more.

From such mechanism, we can conclude that (a) it is impossible to verify, simultaneously, the flow and the stock equilibrium; such system is intrinsically unstable; and (b) long-run expectations (q_1 and q_2) are determined by the short-term adjustment process, the P_o variation. Consequently, this process *is path dependent* Table 1.

This is an important feature for three main reasons:

(i) The equilibrium of the effective demand as it is determined in the GT is a stationary model (Chick 1991, p. 24; Kregel 1976) characterized by stable and exogenous long-run expectations. The method used in the GT is static (Chick 1991, p. 16), and it is the reason why the macroeconomic equilibrium is stable (Asimakopulos 1991, p. 39). *When we relax the hypothesis of stable and exogenous long-run expectations, equilibrium is not stable any more—it is a shifting equilibrium.*

Table 1 Stock and flow equilibrium

Short-run
$P_d > P_o \Rightarrow \nearrow D_k \Rightarrow \nearrow a_1$ e $\nearrow a_2 \Rightarrow \nearrow P_o$;
Flow equilibrium is reached whether $P_d = P_o$ (5)
Stock equilibrium is not realized: $a_1 + q_1 \neq a_2 + q_2 \neq l_3$ (6)
Long run
The system reaches the stock equilibrium:
$\searrow q_1$ e $\searrow q_2 \Rightarrow a_1 + q_1 = a_2 + q_2 = l_3$ (3)
Flow equilibrium is not realized:
$\searrow q_1$ and $\searrow q_2 \Rightarrow \searrow e_1$ and $n \searrow e_2 \Rightarrow \nearrow P_o \Rightarrow P_o > P_d$ (7)

Such equilibrium has been described by Keynes as a "complete dynamic model" (Kregel 1976, p. 215): (a) there is not a predetermined equilibrium, it means no immutable reality (Davidson 1996); (b) such explanation is more complete than the one based on the exogenous animal spirit of the entrepreneurs (Greenwald and Stiglitz 1987). In a post-Keynesian tradition, other authors (Setterfield 1999) reach the same kind of results.

(ii) It is an important feature for the argument developed: as an aggregate quantity of capital is evaluated from the long-run expectations, a change in such expectations implies a change of the value of such quantity of aggregate capital and, consequently of the value equilibrium.

(iii) Finally, this is a fundamental difference in regard to the mainstream, which considers that the cause of the fluctuations is intrinsically exogenous (Davidson 1996): monetary shock for the Rational Expectations Theory, productivity shock or technological shock for the Real Business Cycles Theory, demand shock for the New-Keynesian.[4]

This kind of approach consists in analyzing the impact of a shock on the system. On the contrary, in the Keynesian framework, fluctuations are explained by endogenous variables, which allow us to explain the structural instability of the system (Vercelli 1985, 1991).

From a (post) Keynesian perspective, considering the long-run expectations as exogenous (The animal spirit) implies explaining the investment from a "psychological" shock, by nature exogenous; such analysis does not correspond to the methodological choices that characterize the post Keynesian approach.

[4]In this respect, we must distinguish two kinds of New Keynesians: the first one, represented by authors like Mankiw and Blanchard, shares the neoclassical hard core; the second one, with authors as Akerlof, Grossman and Stiglitz, refutes some components of this hard core. Obviously, the demand shock is used by the first one.

1.2 Specificities of Keynes' Analysis

1.2.1 The Refutation of the Loanable Funds Theory

Such refutation is realized in Keynes' critique of "The Classical Theory of the Rate of Interest," in Chapter XIV of the GT. It may be synthesized in the following way:

$$I = \varphi_1(e - r) \tag{8}$$

$$\varphi_1' > 0$$

$$S = \varphi_3(Y) \tag{9}$$

$$\varphi_3' > 0.$$

(r as the interest rate, I e and S as Investment and Saving, and Y as the product.)

We have two equations and three unknowns, e, r and Y; it is not possible to resolve this system; it is not possible to determinate simultaneously r, *Y and e*. The classical consideration is that Y is exogenous: r and e[5] are determined endogenously and Y *is* determined exogenously in the "real" sphere, by "real" variables.

On the contrary, Keynes considers r as exogenous: "The rate of interest (contrary to what orthodox theory was claiming) must be determined elsewhere by a mechanism which is working (….) *independently*" (Pasinetti 1997, p. 206, italics added). Consequently, Y and e are determined in an endogenous way. *The endogenous determination of e means that* ΣiQi—*the long-run expectations—are partially determined endogenously.* From Eq. (1), we can deduce that, in the long run, a change in e is explained by a change in ΣQi (see Table 1).

[5]From a neoclassical perspective, e is equivalent to the marginal productivity of capital.

As I will demonstrate, economic fluctuations may be explained by fluctuations of the interest rate through the investment multiplier. Does this mean that these fluctuations are the result of an exogenous shock of the interest rate? Does it mean that the Keynesian analysis consists in studying the impact of a shock, by nature exogenous, on the system?

In my opinion, the answer to these questions is no, for the following reasons: r is determined exogenously from the subsystem constituted by the Eqs. (8) and (9). However, with regard to his global framework, Keynes explicitly demonstrates that r is determined from the individual's expectations concerning uncertainty, expressed by their *liquidity preference*. As he writes, the interest rate is "(….) the measure of the unwillingness of those who possess money to part with their liquid control over it" (GT, p. 139). This unwillingness is justified by the existence of strong uncertainty, and by the function of store of wealth assumed by the money (GT, p. 140): the higher the uncertainty, the higher the interest rate to compensate such unwillingness to part with liquidity.

There is a *monetary determination of the interest rate*; as the interest rate determines the investment, monetary variables determine real variables. This is a patent manifestation of the non neutrality of money.

1.2.2 The Aggregation Process

Kregel (1980) builds a dynamical approach from the distinction between capitals with different qualities. Let us consider n kinds of capitals, with decreasing marginal efficiencies: $e_{K1} > e_{K2} > \ldots\ldots\ldots\ldots > e_{Kn}$. The dynamical process may be represented by the following relations:

$$\nearrow D_{K1} \Rightarrow \searrow e_{K1} \text{ until } e_{K1} = e_{K2}$$

$$\nearrow D_{K2} \Rightarrow \searrow e_{K2} \text{ until } e_{K2} = e_{K3}$$

$$\vdots$$

$$\nearrow D_{kn} \Rightarrow \searrow e_{Kn} \text{ until } e_{Kn} = r \ (Dki \text{ as the demand for capital of quality } i)$$

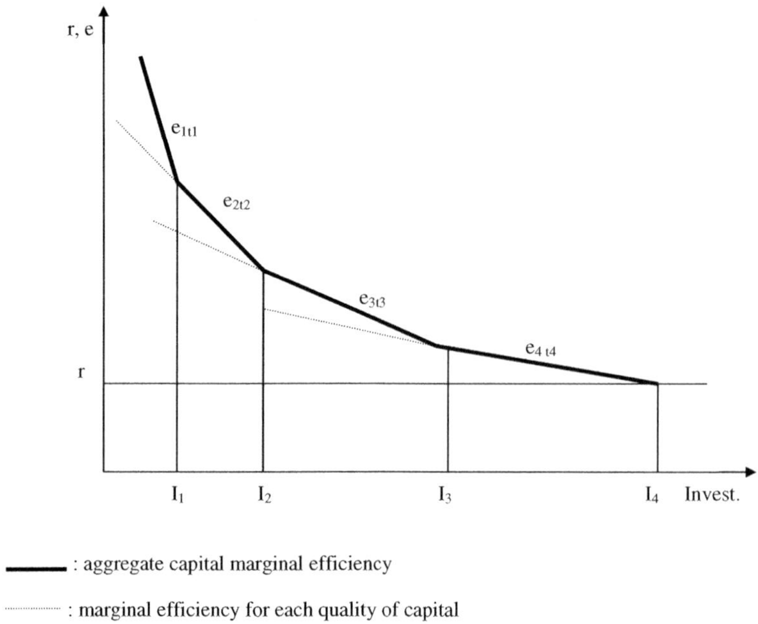

Fig. 1 The aggregate investment function

The equilibrium position is reached when $e_{Kn} = r$. Keynes considers that, for each kind of capital, it is possible to define a curve of marginal efficiency of capital, and that "The greatest of these marginal efficiencies can then be regarded as the marginal efficiency of capital in general" (GT, p. 112). *This means that, in every moment, capitals with different qualities, i.e., different vintages of capital, produce the same return.* This process can be represented as in Fig. 1.

In this example, we can consider four qualities of capital, and suppose that their marginal efficiencies are higher than the interest rate. At time $t_{1,}$ investment in capital with higher quality (K_1 with its corresponding marginal efficiency of capital e_1) will increase until its marginal efficiency becomes equal to $e_{2.}$ Likewise, when capital of quality 1 is exhausted, the demand of capital of quality 2 will increase: consequently, e_2 will decrease until equal to e_3. Such a process will run until the marginal efficiency of the capital of quality 4 is equal to the interest rate.

At each time, the expectations concerning the yields of the investment realized in the past are updated. This is the reason why, during the current period, the overall marginal efficiency of capital is determined by the highest efficiency (GT, p. 112). However, this higher efficiency changes each time, thus allowing us to understand why entrepreneurs today choose a capital with inferior quality: *each time, all kinds of capitals are updated from the current expectations and the returns they provide are the same.*

With regard to Ricardo's theory of differential rent, we can compare the different capitals with the different qualities of land: "Keynes' notion of the marginal efficiency of investment might appear to have some analogy with Ricardo's notion of extensive rent" (Pasinetti 1997, p. 207).

The value of different types of land is updated from the current conditions of profitability. Every period, the capitalist profit on the best quality land is equal to the profit on the other kinds of land. This analysis corresponds to Rotheim's result (1998, p. 370):

> (…) recent research (…..) has shown that Keynes understood diminishing marginal productivity to occur only because of a heterogeneous stock of capital, which had constant returns for any vintage, but whose returns diminished as the margin of utilization spreads to less efficient vintage.

The only difference is that, from my analysis, the return expected of every vintage of capital is not constant during each period.

Keynes uses the same procedure as Ricardo: *the update of the marginal efficiency of the different kinds of capital fulfills the same function as the differential rent of Ricardo*. In Keynes' analysis, the updating process allows for the equalization of marginal efficiencies relative to the different qualities of capital. In the same way, the differential rent allows for the equalization of the capitalist's profits realized on the different qualities of lands. In the two cases, the capitalist will invest in the capital which presents the higher returns, *at this moment.*

2 Keynes' Economics: Structure of the Aggregate Model, Nature of the Capital and Structural Instability

2.1 Keynes and the Aggregation Mechanism

2.1.1 The Neo-Ricardian Premises

On the one hand, Keynes was conscientious of the theoretical difficulties encountered when evaluating and measuring aggregate quantities, principally the national product and the capital, as well as its evolutions. In this respect, he affirms that a "(…) community's output of goods and services is a non-homogenous complex which cannot be measured (…)" (GT, p. 33), and that, when we try to measure the net addition to capital equipment, it is logically impossible "(…) to devise any satisfactory formula to evaluate new equipment against old when, owing to changes in technique, the two are not identical" (idem.).

On the other hand, Keynes "anticipates" the Cambridge Controversy when he highlights the logical incoherency of the neoclassical method, i.e., the logical impossibility to evaluate an aggregate quantity of capital independently of the value of the interest rate: "the attempt to deduce the interest rate from the marginal efficiency of capital is erroneous (…) because the former depends on the scale of the current investment and because we need to know the interest rate to be able to determine this scale" (Keynes 1973, pp. xiv, 477). In this sense, for Keynes, an amount of aggregate capital cannot be conceived as a constant value (Rotheim 1998, p. 375).

Before Keynes, Marshall was aware of such problem. He defined the profit rate as the ratio in which the profit stands to the capital, and affirms that such definition implies "(…) that the money value of the things which constitute the capital has been estimated: and such an estimate is often found to involve great difficulties" (1920, p. 50).

To solve this problem, Keynes will measure "(…) the changes in current output by reference to the number of hours of labor paid for (whether to satisfy consumers *or to produce fresh capital equipment*) on the existing capital equipment, hours of skilled labor being weighted in proportion to their remuneration" (GT, p. 37, italics added). Such definition resembles Smith's commanded labor value theory and is related to the economic meaning of the labor value theory (cf. 1.3.2 Chapter 4).

From a classical perspective inherited from Smith, Ricardo and Marx, Keynes demonstrates that the labor may be conceived as a homogenous measure unit which allows for the measuring of changes in output and in capital. It is the reason why employment is a proxy for real income (Chick 1991, p. 69), since the total quantity of labor is homogenized, i.e., expressed in terms of unskilled labor.

In the neoclassical aggregate model, the natural interest rate "(…) corresponds to the expected return of new equipment, (…) and equals demand and supply for saving" (Wicksell 1987, p. 256). As Wicksell emphasized, the interest rate is determined by real, i.e., not monetary, variables (idem.) in a universe without uncertainty. In such a conception, the value of an aggregate quantity of capital may be calculated regardless of the value of the interest rate; there is no updating of the value of the capital. This procedure is different from that put forth by Keynes and can be explained by the fact that, in the neoclassical macroeconomics, the interest rate and the profit rate are defined as real variables.

This question resembles the Cambridge Controversy concerning the measurement of an aggregate quantity of capital, and the neo-Ricardian developments: every change of the interest rate corresponds to a change in the value of such quantity of capital, which is equivalent to its updating. Such a conception is incompatible with the whole neoclassical framework.

2.1.2 Economic Cycle and Scarcity of Capital

Keynes explains the profit from the scarcity of capital. He defines scarcity of capital as the reason why the return of capital is greater than its supply price: "For the only reason why an asset offers a prospect of yielding having an aggregate value greater than its initial supply price because it is scarce" (GT, p. 180). He then adds "If capital becomes less scarce, the excess yield will diminish, without it having become less productive - at least in the physical sense" (idem.).

The source of the profit is its scarcity. But what is the nature of this scarcity? As noted by Keynes, *scarcity may not be defined in physical terms*. This conception is incompatible with its neoclassical counterpart:

(a) As demonstrated by Pasinetti (1997, p. 207), the marginal efficiency of capital is a concept different from the neoclassical marginal productivity of capital. The former allows us to determine the last profitable investment. It is an *extensive* conception of the investment. On the other hand, the neoclassical conception is defined in an *intensive* way, in terms of capitalistic intensity evaluated from the capital/labor ratio (K/L).
(b) The neoclassical conception is based upon physical quantities of production factors. Implicitly, *this means that it is possible to measure such factors, and that their value is independent of the distributive variables.*
(c) The neoclassical limits of accumulation are physical in nature when comparing the quantity of capital and the quantity of labor. For Keynes, as in Smith and in Marx, such limits are explained by the *social conditions*, and not by the technical or physical ones. The concept of scarcity of capital is present in the Classical Economics. Adam Smith, for example, defined this scarcity in the following manner: "As capital of a country increases, the profits that it can obtain with their employment decrease" (1980, p. 615), in part because wage increase implies in profit decrease (idem., p. 616).

Keynes explains the economic cycle as "(…) cyclical changes in the marginal efficiency of capital (…)" (GT, p. 268). These cyclical changes in the marginal efficiency of capital are caused by abundance or scarcity of capital. In Keynes' conception, the trade cycle is simply the alternation between expansion and recession. Such theoretical approach may explain this alternation between expansion and recession, but despite Keynes' affirmations (Idem), it does not provide an explanation about the temporal regularity of these fluctuations.

Such mechanisms allow for the formulation of an endogenous explanation regarding the cyclical fluctuations: economic fluctuations are produced by endogenous variables: long- and short-run expectations and marginal efficiency of capital.

Finally, within a *dialectical perspective*, Keynes demonstrates that the conditions of the expansion reach economic limits, beyond which they are exhausted. I mean dialectical in the sense of Kalecki (1971) and Marx's (1976). These authors show that the cyclical fluctuation is an endogenous movement,[6] by the fact that, in each phase of the cycle, countertendencies appear and develop. Such mechanism highlights (a) the endogenous character of the cycle, conceived as a *continuous* movement; (b) the existence of a turning point between the different phases of the cycle; and (c) the differences to the neoclassical analysis. Those mechanisms correspond to the Kalecki's analysis of the business upswing (1971) and Marx's analysis of capitalist competition (1976, Livre III, Chapter XV).

During the expansion, the initial conditions disappear progressively, in reference to the increasing abundance of capital. The recession creates the scarcity necessary to produce a new expansion, and so on (GT, p. 268). Based on such mechanisms, I will formalize these relations in a simple model.

The cyclical dynamic presents the following characteristics:

(i) During the expansion phase, the abundance of capital produces an over-investment: this can be defined as "(…) a state of affairs where there is no new investment which is expected (…) to earn in the course of its life more than its replacement costs" (GT, p. 274). Such over-investment may also be explained by the path-dependence between short and long-run expectation. Since short-run expectations partially determine long-run expectations, during the expansion, the increase in short-run expectations implies an increase in long-run expectations, an increase in marginal efficiency of the capital, i.e., an increase in investment. This is the cumulative period of the cycle.

(ii) The initial optimistic expectations which explain the boom "(…) are destined to disappointment" (GT, p. 275), and are

---

[6]In regard to such interpretation, see the concepts of law of motion (Lebowitz 1976, p. 249) and of depreciation of part of social capital (Herscovici 2002, p. 190).

> substituted by pessimist ones. *We observe an endogenous change in the long-run expectations which determine the investment.* This corresponds to the turning point of the expansion phase.

Similar elements are present in the Treatise on Money (1930). In this book, Keynes shows that an excess of saving over investment corresponds to a situation where the entrepreneur's profit is less than the normal profit (GT, p. 67). Keynes builds the following function:

$P = I - S$ (P as the excess of profit, in reference to the normal profit, I and S as the total investment and saving)

If, for example, $S > I$, $P < 0$, i.e., profit is less than normal profit. This situation is characteristic of a recession. On the other hand, if $S < I$, profit is greater than the normal one, and this characterizes a phase of expansion. It is true that in his Treatise, Keynes' argument is made in terms of effective profit, while, in the GT, the argument is built in terms of expected profit.

During the recession, the entrepreneurs reduce the scale of production, while, during the expansion, they increase the scale of production. Consequently, the normal profit may be defined as a situation in which the entrepreneur has no incentive to modify his scale of production: such definition was used by Harrod (1939) to define the warranted growth rate.

Finally, we must note the similarity to Marx's analysis: like Keynes, for Marx, the abundance and the scarcity of capital are not linked to changes in physical labor productivity, but instead with *social conditions of valorization*, i.e., the ratio between surplus value and wages. In this regard, for Marx, expansion leads to over accumulation and over production of capital (1976, Livre III, p. 269). Marx shows that capitalist competition implies the destruction of part of the social capital, so that the other part is able to continue valorizing (in this regard he speaks of *fallowing* of part of social capital). The periodical depreciation of capital corresponds to Chapter 22 of the GT. Marx, much like Keynes, provides an endogenous analysis of the fluctuations, and of the alternation between expansion and recession.[7]

[7] For a simples formalization, see Herscovici (2002, p. 299 and following).

2.2 Structural Instability: The Convergences with the Neo-Ricardian School

2.2.1 The Neo-Ricardian School: Some Methodological Observations

On the one hand, from a post-Keynesian perspective, a predetermined long-period equilibrium is incompatible with the hypothesis of non-ergodicity (Carvalho 1983–1984). On the other hand, the Cambridge Controversy results are incompatible with the existence of a stable long-period equilibrium position, in which the quantity of capital is constant: "*Long-term equilibrium cannot be determined, because the datum relative to the endowment of 'capital' is logically indeterminable*" (Petri 1998, p. 17). As the value of an aggregate quantity of capital changes with a modification of the distributive variables, the long-term equilibrium is undetermined (Setterfield 1999). Moreover, the path dependence between short and long-run variables is incompatible with the existence of a stable, long-period equilibrium. Harrod's model, for example, allows for the formulation of such results (Herscovici 2006).

As previously noted, Chapter XIV of the GT is a crucial component of the Keynesian criticism with regard to the neoclassical framework. The interest rate is determined in an exogenous way, whilst the equilibrium realized is not, systematically speaking, a full employment equilibrium. The neo-Ricardian analysis leads to similar results. In the neoclassical macroeconomics, the perfect flexibility of the interest rate explains the convergence toward equilibrium: the excess of loanable funds demand will be eliminated from an increase of the interest rate. The neo-Ricardian analysis refutes such automatic adjustments:

(a) The Cambridge controversy demonstrates that there is no monotonic relation between the interest rate and the aggregate quantity of capital. Thus, the variation of interest rate does not guarantee the automatic adjustment to the equilibrium position.

(b) On the other hand, the existence of a stable equilibrium is incompatible with such an approach. This equilibrium implies that the quantity of capital must be constant, i.e., it does not depend on the modification of the distributive variables. Such a condition is not verified (Petri 1998, p. 14).

2.2.2 The Structural Instability

We can observe the same type of causal relations in the GT: *the absence of a monotonic relation between the interest rate and the ratio K/L, as well as the absence of a systematic negative correlation between the interest rate and the aggregate quantity of capital.* Let us write:

$$I = \varphi_1(e - r), \text{ with } \varphi_1' > 0 \tag{10}$$

$$\Delta Y = \Delta L = 1/s.\Delta I \tag{11}$$

$$e = \varphi_2(I) \text{ with } \varphi_2' < 0 \tag{12}$$

$$I = \varphi_1[\varphi_2(I) - r] \tag{13}$$

(s is the marginal propensity to save and L is the total quantity of labor).

On the one hand, investment depends on the difference between the marginal efficiency of capital (e) and the interest rate (r). On the other hand, e depends on the stock of capital, i.e., the scarcity or the abundance of capital. Under certain specific conditions, such a system may produce endogenous fluctuations.

(i) If individuals anticipate a reduction of uncertainty, in regard to the liquidity preference, this will cause a subsequent decrease in the interest rate. From (10), we can deduce that the investment will increase. The Keynesian multiplier Eq. (11) will cause an increase in the product and, consequently, in the employment. The hypothesis of Chapter 4 of the GT implies that there is a positive correlation between the variations of the product and the variations of the quantity of labor. If we consider that the variation of labor quantity is, at least, proportional to the product variation, by the multiplier, the increase in Y and L will be greater than the increase in K. The variation of labor (L) will be more than proportional to the variation of the investment, and consequently K/L will decrease. *Contrary to the neoclassical theory, while r decreases, K/L also decreases.*

(ii) From (12), we can deduce that e decreases when I increases. The impact of investment depends on the difference between e and r variations. If decrease in e is bigger than that in r, investment will decrease; in such situation, an initial decrease in r translates into an increase in the K/L ratio.

(i) and (ii) explicitly demonstrate that the *monotonic relation between r and I is not systematically verified in the Keynesian Economics.* This is an important convergence between the Keynesian and the neo-Ricardian framework. From such convergences, I will demonstrate how and why it is possible to deduce that the system produces structural instability in an endogenous way.

(iii) An increase in r will cause, initially, a decrease in I and, a consequent increase in e Eq. (12); if the increase in r is greater than that in e, I will decrease: by the multiplier mechanism, this will cause a recession. During such a recession, decrease in I corresponds to increase in e. This mechanism produces the conditions of a new expansion phase. On the other hand, an exogenous decrease in r has the following implications: an increase in I, and a decrease in e. If the decrease in r is smaller than the decrease in e, this causes, via multiplier mechanism, a recession. In other words, such endogenous fluctuations are due to investment and product fluctuations. Ultimately, fluctuations are caused by a change in the individual evaluations regarding uncertainty. If we introduce temporal lags in Eq. (13), it is possible to obtain chaotic movements with regard to the value of parameters.

$$I_t = \varphi_1\left[\varphi_2(I_{t-1}) - r\right] \tag{14}$$

(iv) Finally, it is possible to highlight the limits of such fluctuations, i.e., the existence of *turning points* in each phase of the cycle. In an expansion phase, the increase of the investment causes a decrease in

> the marginal efficiency of capital. In certain periods, the decrease in *e* will be greater than the decrease in *r*[8]; this results in a recession process, and in the progressive restoration of *e*.

Such mechanisms correspond to the elements of the Chapter 22 of the GT (Notes on the trade cycle): (a) the cycle is produced by endogenous variables; (b) each phase of the cycles corresponds to variations in the marginal efficiency of the capital and in the long-run expectations; (c) contrary to a "mechanical" approach which combines multiplier and accelerator, the fluctuations are not explosive, the countertrend explains the turning point, i.e., the switching between expansion and recession; (d) finally, the initial variation of the interest rate is not a shock, by nature exogenous, but the consequence of a change in individuals' expectations concerning the uncertainty, i.e., *in the liquidity preference.*

Final Remarks

This analysis allows us to affirm that (a) *there is not a monotonic relation between r and K/L*. This is also a neo-Ricardian result; (b) the mechanisms pointed out in the GT allow us to provide an endogenous explanation of economic fluctuations; and (c) it also possible to determine the limits of such fluctuations, from the existence of turning points (GT, p. 274).

Such conception of capital is incompatible with the neoclassical macroeconomic causalities: the distributive variables—the interest rate and the wage rate—are not determined by the market logic, but in an exogenous way; such approach is incompatible with the theory of functional distribution, and these variables are determined by exogenous elements, for example institutions.[9]

From a History of Economic Thought perspective, we can affirm that there is *a methodological and epistemological continuity between Keynes and the neo-Ricardian school.* These two approaches show that there is no

[8]As Keynes did, I suppose that there is an inferior limit of the interest rate (TG, p. 175).

[9]Hodgson (1998, p. 175), for example, shows that wages are not determined by market forces, but from conventions and social institutions. Post-Keynesian authors highlight the role of convention in the determination of the interest rate (Modenesi et al. 2013).

monotonic relation between interest rate and the ratio capital/labor. This is one of the fundamental elements of the refutation of the neoclassical results. *The Cambridge Controversy is the continuity and the generalization of such conception of the capital.* Such a perspective allows us to go beyond the traditional opposition between post Keynesian and neo-Ricardian, and to provide a coherent alternative to the neoclassical paradigm.

One of the most innovative (and perhaps least commented) elements of the GT is the conception concerning the nature of capital. Here is the key point of Keynes' rupture with the "classical" economists. At the same time, such a conception allows us to refute the neoclassical macroeconomics and to design a dynamical alternative. It is no longer necessary to invoke a shock to explain the economic movement; this last point is, in my view, an important step when it comes to building a specifically dynamic analysis.

References

Asimakopulos, Athanasios. 1991. *Keynes's General Theory and Accumulation.* Cambridge: Modern Cambridge Economics.

Barrère, Alain. 1990. *Macroéconomie keynésienne. Le projet économique de John Maynard Keynes.* Paris: Bordas.

———. 1985. Les fondements de l'économie monétaire de production. *Keynes aujourd'hui: théories et politiques*, 35–64. Paris: Economica.

Carvalho, Fernando Cardim de. 1992. Moeda, produção e acumulação: uma perspectiva pós-keynesiana. *Moeda e produção: Teorias comparadas*, 161–191. Brasília: Editora UnB.

———. 1983–1984. On the Concept of Time in Shacklean and Sraffian Economics. *Journal of Post Keynesian Economics* VI (2) (Winter): 265–280.

Chick, Victoria. 1991. *Macroeconomics After Keynes: A Reconsideration of the General Theory.* Cambridge, MA: First MIT Press Edition.

Davidson, Paul. 1978. *Money and the Real World.* London and Basingstoke: The MacMillan Press LTD.

———. 1996. Reality and Economic Theory. *Journal of Post Keynesian Economics* (Summer): 479–508.

Dow, Sheila C. 1985. *Macroeconomic Thought: A Methodological Approach.* Oxford: Basil Blackwell.

Greenwald, B., J.E. Stiglitz. 1987. Keynesian, New Keynesian and New Classical Economists. *Oxford Economic Papers* 39: 119–132.

Harrod, Roy F. 1939. An Essay in Dynamic Theory. *The Economic Journal* 49: 14–33.

Herscovici, Alain. 2002. *Dinâmica macroeconômica: uma interpretação a partir de Marx e de Keynes*. São Paulo: EDUFES/EDUC.

———. 2006. O modelo de Harrod: natureza das expectativas de longo prazo, instabilidade e não linearidade. *Economia e Sociedade* (UNICAMP), Campinas 15 (26): 29–55.

Hodgson, Geoffrey M. 1998. The Approach of Institutional Economics. *Journal of Economic Literature* 36 (1): 166–192.

Keynes, John Maynard. 1930. *A Treatise on Money, Volume I: The Pure Theory of Money*. Edinburgh: Clark.

———. 1973. *The Collected Writings of J. M. Keynes*. London: Macmillan.

———. 2009 [1936]. *The General Theory of Employment, Interest and Money*. New York: Classic Books America.

Kalecki, Michael. 1971. Outline of a Theory of the Business Cycle. In *Selected Essays on the Dynamics of the Capitalist Economy*. Cambridge: Cambridge University Press.

Kregel, J.A. 1976. Economic Methodology in the Face of Uncertainty: The Modelling Methods of Keynes and the Post-Keynesians. *The Economic Journal* 86: 209–225.

———. 1980. Markets and Institutions as Features of a Capitalistic Production System. *Journal of Post-Keynesian Economics* III (1) (Fall): 32–49.

Lebowitz, Michael 1. 1976. Marx's Falling Rate of Profit: A Dialectical View. *The Canadian Journal of Economics* IX (May) (2): 232–454.

Marshall, Alfred.1920. *Principles of Economics*. 8th ed. London: Macmillan and Co, Book II, Chapter IV.

Marx, Karl. 1976. *Le Capital, Critique de l'économie politique*. Paris: Editions Sociales, Livre III.

Modenesi, A., R. Modenesi, J. Oreiro, and N. Martins. 2013. Convention, Interest Rates and Monetary Policy: A Post-Keynesian–French-Conventions-School Approach. *European Journal of Economics and Economic Policies: Intervention* 10 (1): 76–92.

Pasinetti, Luigi L. 1997. The Marginal Efficiency of Investment. In *A "Second Edition" of the General Theory-Vol. 1*, ed. G.C. Harcourt and P.A. Riach, 185–197. London: Routledge.

Petri, Fabio. 1998. The "Sraffian" Critique of Neoclassical Economics: Some Recent Developments. *Revista da Sociedade Brasileira de Economia Política n. 3*, dezembro de: 5–44.

Robinson, Joan. 1983. *Ensaios sobre a teoria do Crescimento Econômico*. São Paulo: Os Economistas [Original: *Further Contribution to Modern Economics*. Oxford, Basil Blackwell Publisher, 1980].

Rotheim, Roy J. 1998. Keynes and the Marginalist Theory of Distribution. *Journal of Post Keynesian Economics* 20 (Spring) (3): 355–387.

Setterfield, Mark. 1999. Expectations, Path Dependence and Effective Demand: A Macroeconomic Model Along Keynesian Lines. *Journal of Post Keynesian Economics* 21 (3) (Spring): 479–501.

Smith, Adam. 1980. *Inquérito sobre a natureza e as causas da riqueza das nações*, vol. I. Lisboa: Fundação Calouste Gulbenkian [Original: *An Inquiry into the Nature and Causes of the Wealth of Nations*. London: Methuen and Co Ltd, 1950].

Vercelli, Alessandro. 1985. Keynes, Schumpeter, Marx and the Structural Instability of Capitalism. In *L'hétérodoxie dans la pensée économique*, ed. G. Deleplace, P. Maurisson org., 279–304, Paris.

———. 1991. *Methodological Foundations of Macroeconomics: Keynes After Lucas*. Cambridge: Cambridge University Press.

Wicksell, Knut. 1987. Lições de Economia Política. In *Os clássicos da Economia*, ed. Ricardo Carneiro org. São Paulo: Ática [Original: *The Influence of Interest Rate on the Prices*. In *Monetarism*, ed. K. Alec Chrystal. London: E. Elgar, 1990].

7

The Relational Economics: An Example of Substantial Hypothesis Refutation

Various studies on the economics of information conducted from the perspective developed by Akerlof, Grossman and Stiglitz support the claim that the signal provided by the market price system is incomplete, particularly with respect to the qualitative components of the goods and services. It is from this *price opacity* that agents will develop opportunistic behaviors, as it becomes impossible to observe certain qualitative variables. This approach, however, is incompatible with the postulates of methodological individualism and the homogeneity of goods and production factors. In this respect, I will show how and from what conditions these asymmetries explain (a) the instability of competition equilibrium and (b) the cumulative nature of the cycle from certain demand externalities.

First, I will highlight the specificities of the economics of information as it was conceived by Stiglitz; this involves emphasizing the incompatibilities between this analysis and the neoclassical analyses from General Equilibrium (GE), whether in the Walrasian or Arrow/Debreu forms or with respect to the theory of rational expectations. Next, using concrete examples linked to labor and financial markets, I will define price opacity and to what extent the current economy is characterized by an intensification of price opacity.

A. Herscovici, *Essays on the Historicity of Capital*,
https://doi.org/10.1007/978-3-030-14838-6_7

The current phase of capitalism is characterized by financial and speculative components; thus, the analysis of these mechanisms is particularly important, and the concept of price opacity appears to be appropriate. On the other hand, such mechanism, as shown before, implies in refuting the substantial hypothesis: the goods value is the result of the agents' relationships, and such relationships move over time. Consequently, historicity is reintroduced in the analysis.

1 Specificities of Information Economics

1.1 Quality Differentiation

1.1.1 Meaning and Implications of Methodological Individualism

The methodological individualism used by the neoclassical SRP implies that individual preferences are objective and that microeconomic functions are fixed. An individual preference is objective when it is exogenous and does not depend on the preferences of other agents (Orléan 2011, p. 58). This hypothesis is incompatible with the existence of externalities, mimetic behaviors, or any strategic behavior that occurs when the behavior of one agent depends on her/his expectations regarding the behaviors of other agents.[1]

An individual preference is fixed when it is not modified during the process of adjustment and choice (idem., p. 77). This characteristic is directly related to the convexity of the individual utility functions, which are required to perform the GE and allows for the understanding of why marginal utility decreases, thus implying that the individual will diversify their basket of goods to maximize its utility. Obviously, these characteristics are not observed if the individual preferences are not fixed. If, on the contrary, an increase in the price of a specific good

[1]Theory of games and oligopoly, for example.

results in an increase in its utility, then such a mechanism contradicts the law of supply and demand and is incompatible with the Pareto optimum.

The adjustment mechanisms toward equilibrium depend directly on this definition of quality. From the moment that quality does not depend either on prices or the action of other agents, the rational agents can maximize their utility function based on two variables: the quantities of goods that constitute the consumer basket and their respective prices (Stiglitz 1987).

The problem of quality is thus partially exogenous: either the problem is not considered because the competitive price system supposedly provides all of the necessary information to the consumer, or it assumes the existence of previous and necessary common knowledge (Arrow 1986, p. 390); however, in this case, it is not possible to assume the methodological individualism hypothesis.

Finally, in such analysis, the agents are price takers; i.e., the price is exogenously determined, and no agent is able to modify it. The rationality of agents is parametric (Orléan, op. cit., p. 89).

The Walrasian competitive market can be defined as a neutral social space within which totally individualized and "independent" agents maximize their utility functions. Let us assume that all of the strategic behavior, or any form of interdependence, is excluded. The Walrasian auctioneer coordinates these independent decisions: he centralizes the purchase intentions, which are expressed as quantities, and allows the determination of the price through which the supply will be equal to the demand. This parabola of auctioneer is a centralizing mechanism; it is the *instantaneous* flexibility of prices that, from this mechanism, explains why exchanges are only so effectively performed when the price corresponds to the equalization of supply and demand.

This mechanism of "*false exchange*" corresponds to the instantaneous equilibrium and to the fact that the decisions of the economic agents are reversible: when the price they announced is different from the equilibrium price, exchanges are not effectively performed. *This conception of equilibrium excludes any form of rationing on the markets* (Stiglitz and Weiss 1981).

1.1.2 Homogeneity and Market Equilibrium

The system of prices provides all of the necessary information related to the quality of goods and services: thus, "(...) objects (...) cannot be distinguished (before purchase) other than by price" (Stiglitz 1987, p. 8). In relation to these qualitative components, it is possible to speak in transparency of the competitive price system; in this sense, in the context of the neoclassical SRP, *prices depend directly on quality* (idem., p. 2). As emphasized by Stiglitz (1987, 2011), the relaxing of this hypothesis is incompatible with the neoclassical SRP, that is, with the efficient markets hypothesis. In the Walrasian matrix, there is supposedly a *homogeneity of goods, services, and production factors.*

Finally, in each market, the law of single price prevails (Stiglitz 1987, p. 8): each good or service with the same set of observed characteristics is sold for the same price.

In relation to prices, the demand curves must have negative slopes, and the supply curves a positive slopes. This law depends directly on the set of hypotheses that are related to, among others, the homogeneity of goods, services, and production factors.

From the moment that information asymmetries emerge and the set of goods and services ceases to be homogeneous, this type of relationship is no longer observed. In the Information Economics (Akerlof 1970; Grossman and Stiglitz 1976, 1980; Stiglitz and Weiss 1981), for uninformed agents, *the quality depends directly on the price*; thus, any increase in the price corresponds to an increase in the demand on the part of the uninformed agents.

With respect to the neoclassical matrix, we have that

$$p = \varphi_1 (Q) \tag{1}$$

The price depends on the quality, the quality is evaluated *objectively* by different agents, and there are no information asymmetries between the producer and the consumer and between the different consumers. The homogeneity of goods and services, using the Walrasian conception, must be interpreted in the following manner: contrary to common sense, this concept does not mean that each type of good or factor has to possess identical qualities, but that *each price corresponds to a specific quality for all of the agents*. There is an "objectification" of quality, and the homogeneity is defined from this *univocal* relationship between price and quality.

In contrast, Stiglitz rejects this objectification and focuses the analysis on the relationships between agents. In opposition, I will qualify such approach as *Relational Economics*[2] to the extent that it primarily studies *the nature of the generalized interdependence of economic agents and its implications*: quality depends on prices, and, as a function of the different information asymmetries, different evaluations of this quality may correspond to the same price. The first mechanism can be formalized from the following relationship:

$$Q = \varphi_2 (p) \tag{2}$$

This type of analysis can be applied to the markets of goods, capital, and labor (Stiglitz 1987, p. 2) and allows formulating the following results: price variation determines a change of the behavior of agents, and this translates into a change in the quality. This is a patent manifestation of this relational economics.

1.2 Information Asymmetries: A Typology

There is no univocal relationship between quality and price. As emphasized by Grossman and Stiglitz (1976), the same variation in prices will be interpreted differently in regard to the dichotomy between informed (i) and uniformed (ui) agents:

$$p = \varphi_3 (Q_i, Q_{ui}) \tag{3}$$

[2] Orléan uses the equivalent term "economy of relationships" (op. cit., p. 22). I could also use the term Behavioral Economics but, to maintain the methodological specificities of this approach and to avoid ambiguities, I prefer to use the term Relational Economics.

These different assessments of quality are obviously incompatible with an "objective" definition of quality and highlight the fact that there is no more univocal relation between price and quality, as shown in Eq. (1).

In the case of experience goods, the same price corresponds to different qualities according to the level of experience of each group of consumers, which leads to the following relationship:

$$p = \varphi_4(Q_{e1}, Q_{e2}, \ldots, Q_{en}) \tag{4}$$

For the same price, each consumer attributes a quality to the good according to their level of experience, e.g., $e_{1,}$ $e_{2,\ldots,}$ e_n.

The asymmetries can be equally defined from the behavior of the different components of supply with respect to quality:

$$p = \varphi_5(Q_1, Q_2, \ldots, Q_x) \tag{5}$$

With respect to the lemon market, Akerlof (1970) clearly shows that identical prices can be equivalent to different qualities, which can lead to the disappearance of that market. The objective heterogeneity of supply is caused by the opportunistic behavior of certain components of the supply, i.e., the "dishonest" sellers.

The efficiency wage confirms this type of relationship. The worker that will be employed at the efficiency wage will increase the quality of the service effectively provided: they will be more "dedicated," and the opportunity cost, if he/she was unemployed, will be greater. Thus, this "loyalty" is translated into greater productivity. The increase in wages corresponds to an increase in the quality of work and their productivity. This may be written as follows:

$$p = \varphi_6(p_i) \tag{6}$$

where $\varphi_6' > 0$.

In the context of this Relational Economics, contrary to the Walrasian construction, the agents are not price takers, and the goods are not homogeneous. Information asymmetries are other manifestations of *heterogenization* of goods and production factors.

1.3 A Parallel with the New Institutional Economics and the Transaction Costs Theory

Stiglitz states that "the information economics paradigm is (...) related to the transaction costs paradigm: indeed, information costs can be viewed as one of the more important categories of transaction cost" (1993, p. 110). I will now demonstrate how the heterogeneity of goods and of the behaviors of agents explains positive transaction costs.

1.3.1 Behavioral Uncertainty and Relational Economics

Information is a public good and, as such, is characterized by its non-exclusivity and non-rivalry. Non-exclusivity means that the agent that produces the information is not able to fully control the modalities of its appropriation: information intrinsically produces *positive externalities* that the different producers cannot appropriate. Non-rivalry is explained by the fact that information is not destroyed by the act of consumption: the consumption of an individual does not imply that other individuals do not consume this good. This emphasizes the *indivisible* nature of the consumption. Knowledge also possesses these characteristics.

Non-exclusivity and non-rivalry make opportunistic behaviors emerge as a function of the possibilities of appropriation of these externalities. In this sense, the *behavioral uncertainty* that characterizes this universe can be assimilated to incomplete information (Barzel 1997, p. 4), and the behaviors of the agents can be assimilated into opportunistic behaviors (Saussier and Yvrande-Billon 2007, pp. 11 and 13). Furthermore, given these multiple possibilities of appropriation of information and knowledge, reverse engineering or simply piracy processes are common. Thus, the system of Property Rights (PR) cannot be fully efficient; using the terminology of Williamson, this means that contracts are, by nature, incomplete. To the extent that contracts are complex (idem.), PR cannot be totally defined neither *self-enforced* (Williamson 2002, p. 188); the implementation of the PR system leads obligatorily to positive transaction costs. The transfer and protection of PR is imperfect and involves positive transaction costs (Barzel 1997, p. 7); the agents that design a contract do not know beforehand the behavior of the different parties nor the implications connected to these behaviors. They do not have full knowledge of the expected returns of the asset (idem., p. 4).

1.3.2 Positive Transaction Costs

Contrary to Walrasian economics, supply and demand are not "anonymous," i.e., they are not composed of homogeneous and substitutable elements. Rather, these relationships are characterized by *bilateral dependence*, as defined by Williamson (2002, p. 175). The choice of a specific modality of governance and the transaction costs that correspond to it depend on, among other things, the specificity of the assets, i.e., a specificity that is "(…) a measure of bilateral dependency (…)" (idem.).

There is a strict relationship between the specificity of goods and the behavior of agents. According to Williamson, assets are specific when they show the following characteristics: irreversibility, heterogeneity, and random valuation. In this respect, Williamson claims that, in this case, "parties to transactions that are bilaterally dependent are 'vulnerable'" (ibid., p. 1760) and that "asset specificity (…) and uncertainty (…) are especially important attributes of transactions" (ibid., p. 180).

The modality of governance will be chosen according to these characteristics and the necessarily positive transaction costs have the objective of decreasing or at least containing this uncertainty. Given that, according to Williamson, contracts are, by nature, incomplete (ibid., p. 188), uncertainty can be decreased but not eliminated. Contrary to the implicit hypothesis used in the Walrasian construction, *enforcement* is not free, nor is it fully efficient (Bowles and Gintis 1993, p. 3).

The economics of information conceived in this manner is totally compatible with the New Institutional Economics, notably with the studies conducted by Coase. In this respect, Stiglitz qualifies the studies of Coase as precursors because they allow emphasizing the importance of institutions on concrete modalities of market functioning (2000, p. 1459). The convergence with the problems developed by

Williamson is equally important because this author demonstrates that contracts are by nature incomplete. Information asymmetries "(...) imply that markets and contracts cannot be complete" and "transaction costs (Williamson 1979) provide the major alternative explanation for incomplete contracts (...)" (Stiglitz 2000, p. 1444).

The choice of a modality of governance depends on the level of transaction costs associated with a specific production and/or a certain quality; there are various modalities of governance, and nothing indicates that the market is the most efficient one (Herscovici 2012). An analysis of this type was performed by Rebitzer (1995) with respect to the concept of efficiency wage. This author compared the gain, in terms of productivity, generated by firms paying a wage above the Walrasian wage with the supervision costs that the firms would have to pay if they did not pay this efficiency wage. From an empirical study of the petrochemical sector and using econometric results, this author concluded that there is a trade-off between wages and supervision costs: "(...) this study finds that high levels of supervision are indeed associated with lower wage levels" (idem., p. 126), which allows for the a priori conclusion that high wages is beneficial to the firms when the increase in wage above the Walrasian wage is compensated by a decrease in the supervision costs and by the increase in productivity.

The problem defines the most appropriate modality of governance, i.e., a governance with high supervision costs and low wages or with high wages and low supervision costs.

2 Price Opacity: An Analysis from the Perspective of the Information Economics

2.1 The Analysis of Grossman and Stiglitz

The paradox of efficient markets was initially stated by Grossman and Stiglitz in their seminal text of 1976; from the moment that part of the information has a cost, it is no longer possible to reconcile the Pareto optimum with the rationality of the informed agents. If the market is competitive, there is a positive externality that results in the information being transmitted freely from the informed agents to the uninformed ones, and the net utility (that is, utility minus the information costs and the price) of the two types of agents is the same. In this case, there is no incentive for the informed agents to buy the information unless the expected net utility is greater than that of the uninformed agents. If this occurs, however, the situation ceases to be Pareto optimal.

In the 1980 text, Grossman and Stiglitz refined the analysis, specifying the impact of the following components on the informative power of the price system: the relative portion of the informed consumers, the cost of information and its quality, the existence of different behaviors and beliefs, and the market size (op. cit., pp. 394 and 395). Nevertheless, the main conclusions are the same as those formulated in the 1976 article: when information has a cost, "(…) there is a fundamental conflict between the efficiency with which the market spreads the information and the incentive to acquire information" (p. 405). Thus, I will use the 1976 text, which I consider to be seminal, and I will complement the analysis with certain elements from the 1980 text.

The 1976 text addresses the quality of a financial asset from the security relative to its financial return. However, this analysis can be applied to the markets of goods, labor, and loans; the quality can be defined, respectively as the real utility of the good, the effective productivity of labor, and the risk exhibited by the debtor in relation to the bank.

Assume that there is a high-risk asset whose return r is equal to:

$$r = \eta + \varepsilon \tag{7}$$

The variable η represents a random variable that can be observed from a specific cost, and ε is a random, unobservable variable: (a) in the case of experience goods, for example, the effective utility of the good will only be known during the act of consumption, (b) when the quality depends on the ex post behavior of agents, this quality will only be known after the completion of the transaction, e.g., the real labor productivity will only be known after the worker has performed his/her task, and received the equivalent of the efficiency wage, and (c) when dealing with credence goods (Herscovici 2018).

The risk[3] that characterizes this asset can be reduced from η, but the uncertainty remains. It is interesting to note that, from this equation, a greater value of ε implies a greater value of r: the return would be a premium to assume the "risk" linked to an asset whose valuation is particularly random. Conversely, a greater value of η indicates a lower risk of the asset and, consequently, a greater value of r. The return r depends on two antagonistic movements: the "risk" associated with the return and, at the same time, its security.

The variables η and ε are independent (Grossman and Stiglitz 1976, p. 246). The variable ε represents the uncertainty as defined by Knight; in this case, the uncertainty cannot be reduced to risk. The absence of futures markets (Grossman and Stiglitz 1980, p. 125) is similar to strong uncertainty: "(...) the events which they (individuals and firms) confront often appear to be unique, and there is no way that they can form a statistical model predicting the probability distribution of outcomes" (idem., p. 31).

The per capita demand of this asset, with respect to the informed agents, depends on the price p and η, which may be written as

$$X_I = X_I(p, \eta) \tag{8}$$

Grossman and Stiglitz state that $\delta X_I/\delta\eta > 0$ and $\delta X_I/\delta p < 0$.

The first relationship implies that a greater value of η results in a greater demand for the asset; in other words, a greater amount of information that reduces risk results in a more secure asset and a greater demand for the asset. The second relationship shows that a higher price results in a lower demand.

$$\lambda X_I(p, \eta) + (1 - \lambda)X_u(p) = X^S \tag{9}$$

The variable λ represents the percentage of informed agents, $(1 - \lambda)$ represents the percentage of uninformed agents, X_{ui} the per capita demand of the uninformed agents, and X^S is the per capita supply of the asset.

The uninformed agents are informed only about the price p; from this observation, that is, from the behavior of the informed agents, they deduce the variations in η: an increase in η implies an increase in the

[3]The risk term in quotation marks corresponds to the uncertainty in the post-Keynesian sense, whereas the same term without quotation marks is related to the probabilistic risk.

demand of the informed agents and, consequently, in p. In this case, each increase in η corresponds to an increase in p; thus, the uninformed agents deduce that η increases equally every time that p increases. In this case, which may be qualified as competitive, the price system generates *positive externalities* from the informed agents to the uninformed agents and transmits all of the information to the uninformed agents; *these externalities negate the information asymmetries and thus explain the equilibrium stability.*

Nevertheless, the price system can transmit a "wrong" piece of information to the uninformed agents. The price p can be increased as a function of the following situations: η is high (*hypothesis 1*), X^s is low (*hypothesis 2*), and the demand is increased (*hypothesis 3*). The signal provided by the price system is "distorted" (noisy signal) by the fact that one cannot systematically relate an increase in η to each increase in p; there is thus opacity in the price system in relation to the information transmitted to the uninformed agents.

From Eqs. (8) and (9), it is possible to deduce that the price depends on the security of the asset and the supply of that same asset. We thus find that:

$$p = p(\eta, X^s) \tag{10}$$

which allows us to write the following equation:

$$\eta = t(p, X^s) \tag{11}$$

Finally, from Eqs. (7) and (11), we obtain:

$$r = t(p, X^s) + \varepsilon \tag{12}$$

Equation (12) shows that, for each given p, the variations in r depend on the variations in X^s and it is impossible to predict ε. More precisely, the uninformed agents deduce the variations in r according to the value of p; however, the variations in r can be equally explained by variations in X^s and not in p.

In these markets, there is interdependence between the supply and the demand: an increase in the supply corresponds to a decrease in the prices. On the part of the uninformed agents, this decrease in the price will be interpreted as an increase in the risk of a given asset, which is translated into a decrease in his demand (Eq. 9).

2.2 The Speculative Dimension

2.2.1 Uncertainty and Speculation

The price system does not transmit information related to the security of the asset. Furthermore, the speculative game and the technological–financial booms (such as that of Nasdaq at the beginning of the 2000s) can be explained by the following mechanism: an increase in p will be interpreted by the uninformed agents as an increase in η, which will generate an increase in demand by the uninformed agents. In view of the particularly random nature of the valuation of these assets, and contrarily to the hypothesis of Grossman and Stiglitz, we can suppose that η and ε *are not independent*: an increase in η, i.e., in the security of the asset, corresponds to a decrease in ε in *the uninformed agents' view.*

This speculative dimension is explained from the introduction of the assessment that the different agents make of uncertainty: ε_i for the informed agents and ε_{ui} for the uninformed agents. For the uninformed agents, an increase in η corresponds to a decrease in ε_{ui}. *In relation to the model of Grossman and Stiglitz, the same increase in the price corresponds to a greater increase in the demand by the uninformed agents.*

It is necessary to clarify that the modification of this hypothesis does not mean that uncertainty can be reduced to risk: the fact that η *and* ε *are not independent simply means that the uninformed agents commit a larger error.* Here, we will consider that each type of agent determines a weighting between the predictable component (η) and the unpredictable component (ε).[4] If ε represents the non-probabilizable part of the

[4]This *démarche* is similar to that developed by Vercelli (1997), who showed how the different agents evaluate the information necessary for the elaboration of probabilities and the lack of this information, i.e., how the agents determine a weighting between the probabilizable and the non-probabilizable parts of the universe.

universe, $|\varepsilon i - \varepsilon|$ *is necessarily less than* $|\varepsilon ui - \varepsilon|$. The error relative to the assessment of the informed agents is, by nature, smaller than that of the uninformed agents because the former does not relate η and ε.

In relation to the reference model, the information asymmetries between agents are more important.

$$X_i = X_i(p,\ \eta,\ \varepsilon_i) \tag{13}$$

Where $\delta X_i/\delta\eta > 0$, $\delta X_i/\delta p < 0$, and $\delta X_i/\delta\varepsilon_i < 0$.

$$X_{ui} = X_{ui}(p,\ \varepsilon_{ui}) \tag{14}$$

Where $\delta X_i/\delta p > 0$ and $\delta X_i/\delta\varepsilon_{ui} < 0$

$$\lambda X_i(p,\ \eta,\ \varepsilon_i) + (1-\lambda)X_{ui}(p,\ \varepsilon_{ui}) = X^s \tag{15}$$

$$p = p\left(\eta,\ X^s,\ \varepsilon_i,\ \varepsilon_{ui}\right) \tag{16}$$

These equations allow one to write:

$$\eta = t\left(p,\ \varepsilon_i,\ \varepsilon_{ui},\ X^s\right) \tag{17}$$

Where *i* and *ui* are related to the informed and uninformed agents, respectively.

The cumulative nature of speculation can be explained in the following manner: an increase in the price corresponds to *an increase in* η *and to a decrease in* ε_{ui} *for the uninformed agents.* This translates into an increase in demand through a new increase in the price and so on.

2.2.2 The Myopia of Uninformed Consumers

The demand of uninformed consumers can be represented in the following manner:

$$X_{ui} = X_{ui}[p,\ (\varepsilon_i - \varepsilon_{ui})] \tag{18}$$

Where $\delta X_{ui}/\delta\ (\varepsilon_i - \varepsilon_{ui}) > 0$ and $\delta X_{ui}/\delta p > 0$.

An increase in p is interpreted by the uninformed agents as an increase in η and a decrease in ε_{ui}; thus, when $(\varepsilon_i - \varepsilon_{ui})$ increases, the demand of the uninformed agents also increases. In contrast, a decrease in $(\varepsilon_i - \varepsilon_{ui})$ represents a decrease in this myopia. i.e., a *decrease in the asymmetries between informed and uninformed agents.*

This myopia explains the increase in demand by uninformed agents and the cumulative nature of this speculative movement. The speculative bubble bursts when the agents realize their "errors." At this point, we again arrive at the same results of Grossman and Stiglitz.

2.3 Sketch of a Theory of the Financial Cycle: Quasi-Equilibrium, Demand Externalities and Cyclical Movement

2.3.1 The Speculative Dynamic

We should establish a parallel between Grossman and Stiglitz's analyses and the Keynesian newspaper competition parable. The mimetic behaviors are linked to general opinion, and they determine the market value; obviously, such behaviors are related to uninformed agents. According to Keynes, the gains are realized by the agents who forecast, sometime before, the behaviors of the majority.

A double mechanism based on *asymmetries and mimicry* is working: asymmetries due to the fact that informed agents forecast, before the uninformed ones, the variations of the asset value—mimicry, because the uninformed imitate the informed ones. An information asymmetry is not defined by occulting information, but by the *temporal lag* between the different agents in terms of access to the "pertinent" information.

We can observe that, contrarily to the neoclassical approach, the universe defined by Grossman and Stiglitz is characterized by temporal lags whilst in the neoclassical universe, such lags do not exist: the adjustment toward equilibrium position occurs *instantly*. In the two universes, the disclosure of information will be effective, but from different temporalities.

It is possible to explain speculative dynamics in the following manner: if η increases, the demand of the informed agents increases, which causes the prices to increase. This increase in prices will be interpreted by the uninformed agents as an increase in η, which explains the increase in their demand; the informed agents decrease their demand. *The process becomes cumulative when the increase in demand by the uninformed agents becomes greater than the decrease in demand by the informed agents.* These conditions are confirmed when a large part of the population is uninformed, for example.

The speculative bubble bursts when the uninformed agents realize their error. During the recession phase, when the prices decrease, uninformed agents sell their assets, and this action explains the cumulative nature of recession. The gains obtained by informed agents are necessarily greater than those achieved by uninformed agents: at the beginning of the financial boom, informed agents purchase the titles when their values are low and sell them after the value are higher. The uninformed agents, on the contrary, buy this asset when the value has already increased and sell it when its value has already decreased, that is, after the financial bubble has already burst: "(…) the informed, on average, buy securities when they are "underpriced" and sell them when they are "overpriced" (relative to what they would have been if information were equalized)" (idem., p. 394).

*The paradox of the efficient markets emphasized by Grossman and Stiglitz (*1976*) is confirmed*: the price system does not allow uninformed agents to deduce the effective variations in η, and the informational advantages of the informed agents translate into higher gains, which confirms the theoretical results obtained in the later model (Grossman and Stiglitz 1980, pp. 394 and 404).

The dynamics of the cycle occurs because a greater error by the uninformed agents results in higher information asymmetries and in a cumulative movement. However, *the heterogeneity of the agents and of their expectations temporality is what explains this cumulative nature and the possibilities of obtaining differential gains.*

Finally, the turning point emerges when the expectations of the uninformed agents are changed, that is, when they modify their expectations. In a stable equilibrium situation, the cyclical movement is nonexistent: the drop in demand of the informed agents compensates the increase in demand on the part of the uninformed agents.

This analysis is completely different from the analyses of financial bubbles performed in terms of rational expectations:

a. the hypothesis of ergodicity is not confirmed, by the fact that the universe is characterized by strong uncertainty;
b. agents interpret information in different manners, which results in different expectations;
c. it is thus impossible to define a fundamental value of the financial asset because its real value is determined from a mechanism of self-fulfillment of prophecies (Orléan 2011, p. 279) without any relationship with the long-term equilibrium value, or with an intrinsic value that would limit the prices variations (Orléan 2011, p. 268, Harrison and Kreps 1978, p. 335); and
d. the cycle has a cumulative nature, which is incompatible with the principle of rational expectations.

The dynamics of the economic cycle may be captured by the following relations:

$$\uparrow D_{it} \rightarrow \uparrow p_{t+1} \rightarrow \uparrow D_{unt+1}\, e \downarrow D_{it+1} \qquad (19)$$

$$\uparrow D_{unt+1} > \downarrow D_{it+1} \rightarrow \uparrow p_{t+2} \rightarrow \uparrow D_a \qquad (19')$$

$$\uparrow D_{unt+1} = \downarrow D_{it+1} \rightarrow p_{t+2} \text{ and } D_a \text{ are constant} \qquad (19'')$$

$$\uparrow D_{unt+1} < \downarrow D_{it+1} \rightarrow \downarrow p_{t+2} \rightarrow \downarrow D_a \qquad (19''')$$

D_{unt+1} and D_{it} as the demand of uninformed and informed agents at period *t*, *pt* the price at period *t* and *Da* the market aggregate demand.

Relation (19′) corresponds to the cumulative phase of the cycle; (19′′) to the stability of the equilibrium. The interpretation of relation (19′′′) is more complex: nevertheless, it shows that the price variation is limited, i.e., non cumulative. This may be interpreted as oscillations from a long-term equilibrium value.

2.3.2 Expectations Heterogeneity and Quasi-Equilibrium

2.3.2.1 Expectations Heterogeneity and Aggregation Modalities

Let us express the demand per capita of informed agents by:

$$D_i = \varphi_1(\eta, p) \tag{20}$$

with $\delta\varphi_1/\delta\eta > 0$, and $\delta\varphi_1/\delta p < 0$

and the demand per capita of uninformed agents by:

$$D_{un} = \varphi_2(p) \tag{21}$$

with $\delta\varphi_2/\delta p > 0$

λ as the relative share of informed agents; and β $(1 - \lambda)$ as the relative share of uninformed agents. The aggregate demand in the market (Da) may be expressed by:

$$D_a = \lambda\varphi_1(\eta, p) + \beta\varphi_2(p) = D_i + D_{un} \tag{22}$$

Equilibrium stability or, to the contrary, cumulative cycle, depends on β value. If β is low, most part of the agents is informed: the differential gains are lower and the price variations satisfactorily express the demand of informed agents. For example, a lower information cost may explain such situation: the market is transparent, uninformed agents benefit from the positive externalities generated by the informed ones, and markets are relatively competitive. I will qualify this situation as a competitive *quasi-equilibrium*. If price system conveys information to the uninformed agents, all agents are informed.

2.3.2.2 Equilibrium Instability and Cumulative Mechanisms

In a quasi-equilibrium situation, β is close to one or zero (ibid., p. 395). If all agents are informed, or if no one is informed, all agents will develop the same expectations, and market will disappear: "(….) *the creation of markets eliminates the differences of beliefs that gave rise to them and thus causes those markets to disappear*" (ibid., p. 404).

If β is close to 1, some agents will realize that they can increase their gains by getting informed; β will decrease, a cumulative process appears, which shows, without any ambiguity, that this quasi equilibrium is not stable. Equilibrium stability implies that β varies between some critical values, to verify (19′′) and (19′′′). If β is close to 0, most part is informed: nevertheless, opportunistic behaviors will appear and develop, i.e., part of the agents will become uninformed; β will increase, as well as D_{un}, and the cycle will get cumulative. *Endogenous variations of* β allow explaining the existence of the cumulative phase of the cycle, as well as the turning point, i.e., the tendency reversion.

The Explicative Variables

The modification of the externalities nature is a key element to explain this dynamics: positive externalities produced by informed agents are endogenized by uninformed ones. ***Ext. 1*** correspond to the equilibrium stability and to the reduction of information asymmetries. On the contrary, positive externalities produced by the uninformed (***Ext. 2***) characterize the cumulative phase and implies an increase of the information asymmetries.

This model allows designing an endogenous explication of the development of expectations and explaining (a) why *expectations heterogeneity* is a necessary condition for the existence of a cyclical movement and (b) how the heterogeneity degree of such expectations changes during the different phases of the cycle. *The cyclical movement is explained by the modification in the nature of externalities*: the equilibrium rupture, the cumulative processes, the turning point and the trend reversion.

As demonstrated, the speculative dynamics is explained by mimetic and differentiated behaviors. Uninformed agents forecast, *with a temporal lag*, the tendency reversions, in relation to the informed agents. Asymmetries will be defined from such lags: the information disclosure is the same for all kind of agents, but the disclosure temporality is different: the informed agents, i.e., the speculators can "(…) anticipate the basis of conventional valuations a few months hence (…)" (GT, p. 129).

2.3.2.3 The Different Phases of the Cycle

The Initial Equilibrium

Let us suppose that, initially, the system is balanced. If, for example, β is close to 0, nearly all agents are informed; opportunistic behaviors will appear, and part of the individuals will not be informed anymore; β will increase until some critical value V_1. While externalities Ext. 1 work, equilibrium is stable. When β exceeds V_1, the nature of externalities change and the system becomes unstable (cf. [19′′]) (Fig. 1).

The Cumulative Process

During this cumulative phase, D_{unt} variations are greater than D_{it} variations and β increases. While it continues inferior to V_2, the process continues cumulative.

Turning Point and Trend Reversal

When β becomes greater than V_2, the process is not cumulative any more. The uninformed agents "realize their mistake" and change their expectations, in an opposite way. The externalities nature changes too; β will decrease, and *information is spreading*. This dynamics leads to a crisis and to a trend reversal.

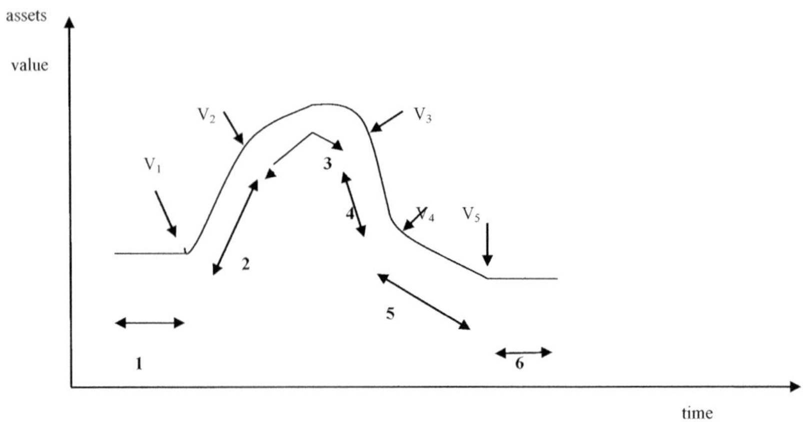

Fig. 1 The different phases of the cycle

The same processes will work in the opposite direction during the other phases: V_3 is the critical value from which the recession becomes cumulative, V_4 the new turning point and V_5 the point from which the system becomes stable.

This analysis corresponds exactly to the mechanisms pointed by Grossman and Stiglitz:

i. It provides an endogenous explication in regard to the determinations of the expectations, and to its modifications. We should note that during different phases of the cycle, the heterogeneity degree changes.
ii. Equilibrium is intrinsically unstable and during the different phases of the cycles, the Pareto conditions are no verified.
iii. From such approach, we can explain the trend reversal and the transition between expansion and recession; we can complement Orléan's analysis (2011) by explaining the turning point and the trend reversion (Table 1).

2.3.3 Some Methodological Implications

It is equally important to note that the analysis by Stiglitz constitutes a radical criticism of neoclassical economics through the refutation of the existence of a fundamental value: in regard to the financial markets, from the efficient market theory, as developed by Fama (1998) or Tirole (2016), for example, the price system provides *instantaneously* the same information for all the agents (Malkiel 2003). There is no place for speculation mechanism, neither for temporal lags in regard to the access to the pertinent information, or divergences in regard to the interpretation of the same information. The main difference in regard to the mainstream interpretation is related to the velocity in which the price system discloses information: from the mainstream perspective, disclosure is instantaneous whilst, in Stiglitz's approach, such disclosure takes some time; this is necessary and sufficient to explain the information asymmetries and the speculative mechanism.

Table 1 The speculative cycle

Equilibrium (1)	Cumulative process (1)	Turning point (1)	Cumulative process (2)	Turning point o (2)	Equilibrium (2)
$V_1 > \beta \geq 0$	$V_2 > \beta \geq V_1$	$V_3 > \beta \geq V_2$	$V_4 > \beta \geq V_3$	$V_5 > \beta \geq V_4$	$_{xxxx} > \beta > V_5$
$\beta \approx 0$	$\uparrow \beta$	$\downarrow \beta$	$\uparrow \beta$	$\downarrow \beta$	$\beta \approx 0$
Information					
Imperfections					
$\mapsto$ free riders	Phase 1	Phase 2	Phase 3	Phase 4	Phase 5
$\Rightarrow \uparrow \beta$					
Ext. 1	Ext. 2	Ext. 1	Ext. 2	Ext. 1	Ext. 1
	$\uparrow$ asymmetries	$\downarrow$ asymmetries	$\uparrow$ asymmetries	$\downarrow$ asymmetries	
		Info. disclosure		Info. disclosure	

On the other hand, the fundamental value is conceived as the regulatory variable of these financial markets: when the divergence between the market price and this fundamental value increases beyond some critical level, the financial bubble bursts. But the fundamental value cannot be conceived as a regulatory variable, insofar as its evolutions may be chaotic, in regard to the changes in information.[5]

In the neoclassical analysis, the causes of the financial fluctuations are, by nature, exogenous; we can speak here in *an informational shock*, by nature exogenous. The existence of this fundamental value is equivalent to the refutation of what I defined as speculative finance: this means that *the only function of finance is to finance the productive sector.*

On the contrary, the Information Economics initiated by, Keynes, Akerlof, Grossman and Stigliz, allows formulating other results: in the absence of a fundamental value, the effective value is determined by social relationships, and its implications in terms of expectations elaboration; such mechanisms are *endogenous.* We can observe that the dynamic of the cycle is explained by the information asymmetries; such asymmetries appear in relation to the different temporality of disclosure of information between the different types of agents. Consequently, the price system does not convey all information for all agents, and does not allow realizing a perfect coordination on the markets.

Finally, as I demonstrated, the instability of the equilibrium depends on the importance of information asymmetries: the most important are the asymmetries, the most important is the instability of the equilibrium.

Final Observations

In conclusion, as emphasized in this chapter, one can state that the current phase of the capitalist system (the financialization of capitalism) is characterized by an increase in the opacity of the price system. In a recent article, Stiglitz (2011) formulates a similar conclusion and states that there is an increase in information asymmetries and in the speculative dimensions of all markets.

---

[5]Such mechanism is representative of the random walk of this fundamental value.

In the competitive market, uninformed agents benefit from positive externalities generated by informed agents (Grossman and Stiglitz 1976, 1980); the demand externalities fulfill a stabilizing role because they negate the effects of information asymmetries between informed and uninformed agents. In contrast, in speculative markets, which are characterized by important information asymmetries, informed agents benefit from the positive externalities generated by the uninformed agents, which translate into the broadening of information asymmetries that explain the cumulative nature of the different phases of the cycle.

Stiglitz's approach no longer involves studying the problems of information from the Walrasian matrix, but rather constructing an alternative paradigm. In this alternative paradigm, the function of the price system is not providing information related to the scarcity of goods, but rather information related to the qualitative characteristics of the goods and the behaviors of the agents (Stiglitz 2000, pp. 1447 and 1469). This makes it necessary to redefine the object of Economic Science. Contrary to the traditional definition, this object can no longer be defined as the study of mechanisms that allow the efficient allocation of scarce resources from the price system; instead, it has to include the economic and institutional structures that determine "(….) the ability to create, transmit, absorb, and use knowledge and information" (Stiglitz 2000, p. 1471).

References

Akerlof, G. 1970. The Market for "Lemons": Qualitative Uncertainty and the Market Mechanism. *Quarterly Journal of Economics* 89 (August): 488–500.

Arrow, Kenneth J. 1986 [1974]. Rationality of Self and Others in an Economic System. *The Journal of Business* 59 (4): 385–399.

Barzel Yoram. 1997. *Economic Analysis of Property Rights*. Cambridge: Cambridge University Press.

Bowles, Samuel, and Herbert Gintis. 1993. The Revenge of Homo Economicus: Contested Exchange and the Revival of Political Economy. *The Journal of Economic Perspectives* 7 (1): 83–102.

Fama, E. 1998. Market Efficiency, Long Term Returns and Behavioral Finance. *Journal of Financial Economics* 49 (3): 283–306.

Grossman, S.J., and J.E. Stiglitz. 1976. Information and Competitive Price system. *The American Economic Review* 66 (2) (May): 246–253.

———. 1980. On the Impossibility of Informationally Efficient Markets. *The American Economic Review* 70 (3) (June): 393–408.

Harrison, M.J., and D.M. Kreps. 1978. Speculative Investor Behavior in a Stock Market with Heterogeneous Expectations. *Quarterly Journal of Economics* XCIII (2): 323–336.

Herscovici, Alain. 2012. Informação, conhecimento e Direitos de Propriedade Intelectual:os limites dos mecanismos de mercado e das modalidades de negociação privada. A contribuição de Williamson à análise dos Direitos de Propriedade Intelectual [Information, Knowledge and Intellectual Property Rights: The Limits of Market Mechanisms and Private Negotiation. The contribution of Williamson to the Analysis of Intellectual Property Rights]. *Economia e Sociedade, Campinas* 21 (3) (46) (December): 667–694.

———. 2018. Assimetrias da informação, qualidade e mercados da certificação: a necessidade de uma intervenção institucional. *Revista de Economia Contemporânea* 21: 5–18.

Keynes, John Maynard. 2009 [1936]. *The General Theory of Employment, Interest and Money*. New York: Classic Books America.

Malkiel, B.G. 2003. The Efficient Market Hypothesis and Its Critics. *Journal of Economic Perspectives* 17 (1): 59–82.

Orléan, André, 2011. *L'empire de la valeur. Refonderl'Économie* [The Empire of Value. Rebuilding the Economy]. Paris: Éditions du Seuil.

Rebitzer, James B.B. 1995. Is There a Trade-Off Between Supervision and Wages? An Empirical Test of Efficiency Wages Theory. *Journal of Economic Behavior and Organization* 28: 107–129.

Saussier, Stéphane, and Anne Yvrande-Billon. 2007. *Économie des coûts de transaction* [Transaction Cost Economics]. *La Découverte*, Paris.

Stiglitz, Joseph E. 1987. The Causes and Consequences of the Dependence of Quality on Price. *Journal of Economic Literature* XXV (March): 1–48.

———. 1993. Post Walrasian and Post Marxian Economics. *The Journal of Economic Perspectives* 7 (1): 109–114.

———. 2000. The Contribution to the Economics of Information to Twentieth Century Economics. *The Quarterly Journal of Economics* 115 (November): 1441–1478.

————. 2003. Information and the Change in the Paradigm in Economics, Part 1. *American Economist* 47 (Fall): 6–26.

———. 2011. Rethinking Macroeconomics: What Failed and How to Repair It. *Journal of the European Economic Association* 9 (4): 591–645.
Stiglitz, Joseph E., and Andrew Weiss. 1981. Credit Rationing in Markets with Imperfect Information. *The American Economic Review* 71 (3): 393–410.
Tirole, Jean. 2016. *Economie du bien commun*. Paris: PUF.
Vercelli Alessandro. 1997. *Liquidity Preference and Option Values*. Preliminary Draft, manuscript.
Williamson, Oliver E. 2002. The Theory of the Firm as Governance Structure: From Choice to Contract. *Journal of Economic Prospectives* 16 (3) (Summer).

8

The Problem of the Empirical Data: Capital in the Twenty-First Century?

In this chapter, I will make a critical and methodological analysis of the theses presented by Piketty in his book "Capital in the twenty first century" (2014). If, as noted by Ricardo, the main problem of political economy is to determine the laws that regulate the distribution of income among different social classes, the study of such mechanisms must be supported by a theoretical background which defines a value theory and/or the nature of capital. The whole modern epistemology (Popper, Kuhn and Lakatos) refutes the positivism and demonstrates that reality observation is, by nature, interpreted within a theoretical matrix.

Income distribution and long-term growth are linked to the specificities of capital and/or to the choice of a value theory: in Ricardo's theory of differential rent, for example, heterogeneity of land determines the income distribution, whereas, deriving out of homogeneous capital, neoclassical theory explains income distribution encompassed by a traditional production function. *The definition of the nature of capital and/or the choice of a value theory are the necessary conditions to explain the modalities of growth and income distribution.* In this regard, Piketty discards the Cambridge Controversy, from empirical arguments (2014, p. 167). The empiric data cannot constitute an epistemological criterion per se. This debate occurs at a theoretical level, and the arguments must be theoretical ones.

A. Herscovici, *Essays on the Historicity of Capital*,
https://doi.org/10.1007/978-3-030-14838-6_8

Piketty's approach discards the social and historical dimension of capital: if we consider economic anthropology and economic history approach (Marx, Braudel, Dumont and Polanyi), it is possible to affirm that capital is a social mechanism limited to capitalism, and it cannot be extended to other modes of production. Piketty considers capital as supra-historical. This means that social relations and modalities of expectations elaboration are "immutable." We can speak in capital *reification*: capital is not conceived as a social and historical relation, but as a "thing" whose qualitative characteristic does not change over time.

From the Neo-Ricardian and Keynesian framework, distribution variables, and/or expectations determine the value of an aggregate quantity of capital. Although Piketty invokes classical and Keynesian authors, he deduces income distribution from capital evaluated as "quantities"; in regard to a Keynesian and/or Neo-Ricardian perspective, I will demonstrate why Piketty's argument is fallacious.

I will formulate three kinds of criticisms: the first one comes from Economic History (Braudel 1979, 1985; Polanyi 1983), Economic Anthropology (Dumont 1985) and Institutional Economics (Orléan 2011); the second one, from the Cambridge tradition, mainly from Ricardo, Marx, Keynes and Sraffa. The third one is related to the fact that Piketty does not adopt a specific theoretical matrix and mixes various incompatible methodological frameworks. Consequently, his empirical observations are not, in most part, theoretically coherent.

In Part I, I will present the framework designed by Piketty and his main results. In Part II, I will highlight the absence of History and the methodological problems present in Piketty's démarche.

1 Piketty's Thesis: A First Approach

1.1 The Two Fundamental Laws of Capitalism

1.1.1 The First Fundamental Law

The first fundamental law is represented by the following equation (Piketty 2014, p. 42):

$$\alpha = r \cdot \beta \tag{1}$$

where α is the share of income from capital in the national product, β is the capital/income ratio (the capital coefficient) and r is the rate of return on capital.

This equation shows, without any ambiguity, that *income distribution is determined from the quantities of capital.* The increase of β, from the law of decreasing marginal product, implies that the marginal productivity of the capital decreases. As observed by Solow (2014), the variation of α depends on the relative variations of r and β. If the decrease of r is proportionally less important than the increase of β, α will increase.

The impact of the increase of β on the share of income on capital in the product depends on the substitution elasticity of the production factors. In the aggregate production function used by Solow in his seminal model (1956), such elasticity is equal to one: the decrease of r is compensated by the increase of β, and the share of income from capital (and from labor) is constant. The verification of Piketty's result, i.e., the increase of α, in the long run, implies in substitution elasticity higher than one. Piketty does not justify such hypothesis. But once adopted, from Eq. (1), in a mechanical and tautological manner, the share of profit will increase.

We must note that such observations only apply to productive capital, i.e., to capital used directly in production. However, Piketty invokes the Ricardian theory of differential rent to justify his thesis (2014, p. 11). He establishes the following parallel: according to Ricardo, the concentration of income is explained by the ownership of land. In Piketty's analysis, such concentration is explained by the capital ownership. *Such parallel is partial and fallacious*:

– In Ricardo's theory, the scarcity of the lands of best quality explains the increasing land ownership's share of income. Such rent is explained by scarcity and, as Ricardo demonstrates, is totally unproductive. *The Ricardian concept of scarcity can only be applied to patrimonial and eventually to speculative capital.* On the other hand, *the law of diminishing returns can only be applied to productive capital.* This highlights the limits of applicability of Eq. (1) and the limits of Piketty's hypothesis related to substitution elasticity of production factors.

- In the classical, the neoclassical and the Keynesian tradition, the tendency to decrease profit rate is explained by the abundance of productive capital: the economic development for Ricardo (1821), the increase in the organic composition of capital for Marx, the decreasing diminishing returns law for the neoclassical school, and the decrease of the marginal efficiency of capital for Keynes. This means that, *in Piketty's analysis, the decrease in the profit rate of productive capital would be compensated by the increase of return obtained from the other kinds of capital.*

This mechanism shows explicitly that the income concentration is not due to the capitalist, i.e., the owners of productive capital, but to the rentiers, i.e., the owners of patrimonial and speculative capital.[1] But are these other kinds of capital scarce, from a qualitative and quantitative criterion? There is a neither empirical nor theoretical robust evidence to confirm the existence and the intensification of the scarcity of such kind of capital in the long run. On the contrary, the financialization of economies translates abundance of financial capitals. Nevertheless, scarcity is the necessary and sufficient condition to support Piketty's thesis.

1.1.2 The Second Fundamental Law

$$\beta = s/g \tag{2}$$

(s is the saving rate, g is the income increase rate and β is the capital/income ratio)

The saving rate s determines the capital coefficient. So, in the long run, investment is funded by saving (Piketty 2014, p. 144). This is a long-run law that will be achieved only tendentiously. Such law is

[1]See Marwil-Dávila and Oreiro (2016).

valid only if "asset prices evolves on average the same way as consumer prices" (idem., p. 122): (a) there is not theoretical justification to validate such hypothesis and (b) *In regard to a Neo-Ricardian approach, this implies that the ratio capital/labor (the organic composition of capital) is the same in the capital production and consumer goods production sectors. And there is no reason to verify this hypothesis.* If asset prices increase proportionally more than consumer goods, β will increase regardless of s.

Piketty interprets Harrod basic equation in the following way:

$$g = s/\beta \tag{3}$$

If β is constant, as supposed by Harrod, the rate of income increase is entirely determined by the saving rate. Instability is explained by the impossibility to verify (3). This is an erroneous interpretation: the Harrodian instability is explained, in the short run, from the discrepancy between the rate of increase of the real income and the warranted rate, and in the long run from the discrepancy between the natural rate of increase of income Gn and the warranted rate (Harrod 1939; Herscovici 2006a). On other hand, there is path dependence: the long-term position depends on the short-term fluctuations (Besomi 2001).

a. From a Keynesian perspective, it is not possible to affirm that the saving rate determines the level of the product. Saving is a determinate and not a determinant variable (Chick 1991, p. 189): "Saving, like consumption, depends on current income, so (…) it cannot initiate a change in income (…)."
b. The fact to suppose that β is constant may not be justified from technological specificities, as Piketty supposes[2] (Piketty 2014, pp. 165 and 166).
c. Solow's model (1956) corresponds to the following equation:

---

[2]See our discussion in Chapter II.

$$\beta = s/g \qquad (3')$$

The capital coefficient is determined by the rate of saving. β is no longer constant and adjusts to the value that corresponds to the balanced growth path from s variation. In Solow's model (1956), adjustment mechanism toward the steady-state position is based on such relation.

This relation is totally incompatible with Harrod's perspective: on one hand, in Solow's model, the factors substitution allows to realize the convergence toward the steady-state position. On the other hand, saving determines this long-run convergence process. Such causality implies in validating the loanable funds theory and all the causal structure of neoclassical macroeconomics (Herscovici 2006b).

From (1) and (2), we can deduce that:

$$\alpha = r.s/g \qquad (4)$$

The rate of return on capital and the saving rate determine the share of income from capital in the national product. Such mechanism is based on the active role of saving.

Finally, the smaller the g, the higher the α: periods with a weak rate of increase of national income correspond to an increase in the relative share of income from capital. This corresponds to the stylized facts, from 1990 until today.[3]

In regard to the inverse relationship between abundance of capital and return rate, we must deduce that the decrease in return rate on capital is compensated by an increase relatively more important in capital value, i.e., in β. One more time, we are confronted (a) with the problem of the historical evolution of the value of different quantities of aggregate capital and (b) with the heterogeneity of such capital and of such return rates.

[3]For an alternative analysis, see Marwil-Dávila and Oreiro (2016).

1.2 The Main Concepts: Definition and Theoretical Framework

1.2.1 The Capital

Piketty defines capital as "all forms of real property (including residential real estate) as well as financial and professional capital (plants, infrastructure, machinery, patents, and so on) used by firms and government agencies" (Piketty 2014, p. 36). Such definition includes financial capital, capital used directly in productive activities, and all forms of immaterial capital.

Such definition is essentially *patrimonial* and directly related to the concepts of wealth and property. From such perspective, capital is equivalent to wealth (idem.). This definition is "weak" for the following reasons: capital is a heterogeneous aggregate and, from a theoretical and empirical approach, we are confronted to the problem of the measurement of an aggregate quantity of capital.

The theoretical problem was systematized by Ricardo, Sraffa and the Neo-Ricardian school, and led to the Cambridge controversy; this theoretical debate cannot be resolved based on empirical data. In this respect, Piketty affirms that "the virulence—and at times sterility — of the Cambridge capital controversy was due in part to the fact that participants on both sides lacked the historical data needed to clarify the terms of the debate" (idem., p. 167). Such simplistic positivism does not allow ignoring the debate that starts with Ricardo, goes on with Marshall and Keynes, and is systematized with Sraffa and the Neo-Ricardian school:

i. First, it is not possible to study data without a referential theoretical matrix. This contradicts all the modern epistemology results, from Popper to Lakatos. It is not possible to realize an observation and a classification of data independently from a theoretical framework. In this respect, Lakatos demonstrates that a progressive Scientific Research Program is characterized by the fact that theoretical development must anticipate the empirical one (Lakatos 1978, p. 79); the systematic use of the inductive method to justify hypothesis, as Piketty does, is characteristic of a degenerative program.

ii. Secondly, the heterogeneity of capital involves the problem relative to the construction of tools that allow measuring quantities of aggregate capital and its evolutions in the long run. Neoclassical production functions conceive the aggregate capital as a quantity; the income distribution is conceived as the contribution of production factors to the product. The negation of the Cambridge controversy allows Piketty to deduce, as neoclassical school does, the income distribution from the quantities of factors and to interpret the data from such neoclassical framework. The empirical observations and Piketty's economic laws depend on such premises[4] and his results are the logical consequence of assimilation of quantities and values.

In Chapter V, *I demonstrated that it is possible to assimilate quantities and values only when capital is homogenous*. Empirical results would be totally different if Piketty would use other hypothesis. To solve this problem, he proposes to evaluate all forms of wealth in terms of market prices at a given point in time (Piketty 2014, p. 108). This resolution is particularly incomplete: how is it possible to compare market prices of productive capital, financial capital and "patrimonial" capital? The modalities of determination of prices are different and specific for each type of capital. Markets for intangible and financial capital are particularly unstable: beyond this instability, is it possible to draw a long-run tendency?

1.2.2 The Determination of the Rate of Return

The rate of return of the capital is defined by the ratio between the capital return during a given period and the value of the capital invested (idem., p. 93).

---

[4]In respect to the theoretical an empirical limits of such approach, see J. Felipe and J. S. L. McCombie (2005).

i. *To what extent is it possible to apply the same rate of return to heterogeneous capital?* The return of productive capital is the profit rate, the return of the financial capital, in its speculative dimension, is fundamentally the corresponding variations of its value. If some kind of capital is determined in function of the use value (family patrimony, for example), what is the meaning of a rate of return applied to such capital?

Keynes made this kind of differentiation between speculative investments and productive ones: the former are related to the short run, do not work for the general interest, and its return depends on the information asymmetries, the latter presents the opposite characteristics (GT, p. 132).

In Chapter XVII of the General Theory (p. 188), Keynes demonstrates that there is a specific rate of interest for each kind of capital. For example, if the spot value of 100 quarters of wheat is £100 and the forward value of the same quantity £105, for one year, "(...) the 'wheat- rate of interest' is 5 per cent per annum" (idem.). Now, let us suppose that the forward value of 100 quarters of wheat is £107, and the money-rate interest 5%. The "wheat- rate of interest of money" is minus 2% per annum: it allows buying 98 (105/107) quarters of wheat in the future. Consequently, Keynes affirms, in regard to commodities, that "(...) there is no reason why their rates of interest should be the same for different commodities" (idem., p. 89). *The rate of return is different for each commodity and for each capital.* Such mechanism may be applied to the method used by Piketty, as he evaluates the returns on capital.

ii. The second problem is related to the relationship between the (monetary) rate of interest and the profit rate. According to Piketty, the rate of return on capital is "(...) a broader notion than the 'rate of profit,' and much broader than the 'rate of interest,' while incorporating both" (ibid., p. 42); this means that the determinant variable is the rate of return on capital, and not the monetary rate of interest.

In Chapter IV, in regard to speculative markets, I demonstrated that at each kind of capital correspond specific yields; the return of productive finance depends on the interest rate, in a long-term perspective, the return of speculative finance on the variation of the value of the assets in the short term, and the return of the productive assets on the marginal efficiency of capital, in the long term. The dynamic and the temporalities are different for each kind of capital.

More specifically in regard to the speculative capital, the instability of its value is particularly important, and such instability is the main component of the speculative activities; contrarily to Piketty's attempts, such value instability does not allow the temporal comparison in the long run.

Both the Classical/Cambridgean and the Keynesian economy conceptions allow refuting Piketty's affirmation.

According to Keynes, each asset depends on four attributes: *q*, the expected yield, *c* the carrying cost and *l* the liquidity-premium (GT, p. 191). If *a* is the expected appreciation of the asset in terms of itself, the return of each asset is equal to $(q-c+\text{l}+a)$. If we consider, for example, two productive assets and the money, the stock equilibrium implies that the return of each asset is equal:

$$q_1 + a_1 = q_2 + a_2 = l_3 \tag{5}$$

(assets 1 and 2 are productive assets and asset 3 is the money).

Equation (5) expresses the equilibrium conditions: in this situation, the rates of return of the different assets are equal. If the rate of return of one kind of capital is higher than the other rates of return, equilibrium will be broken; capital will be invested in the sector that presents the higher rate of return.

a. On the one hand, the Keynesian dynamic may be explained in the following way: if the rate of return of a capital *x* is higher than the rates of return of other kinds of capital, such situation implies an increase of its demand and in a decrease in *x* marginal efficiency, in regard to short- and long-run mechanisms (GT, Chapter 11). Such mechanism will work until *x* marginal efficiency is equal to the rate of return of the other capitals, i.e., to verify the equilibrium conditions.

b. On the other hand, the return rate of money is defined by the liquidity premium; its marginal efficiency does not decrease systematically (Kregel 1980) when its demand increases. It is the reason (a) why the money-rate of interest is the greatest (GT, p. 189) and (b) why it will be determinant in the investment decision.
c. Why doesn't the marginal efficiency of money (the interest rate) decrease when its demand increases? This may be explained by the role of store of wealth assumed by the money: if the liquidity preference increases proportionally more than the supply of money, the rate of interest will increase (GT, p. 144). We must observe also that the rate of interest is determinate in an exogenous way (Vercelli 1991; Pasinetti 1997, p. 209); this conception is totally different from the natural rate of interest determined by the loanable funds theory.
d. Investment depends on the difference between the return of capital and the return of money, i.e., the monetary rate of interest. When the return of capital (or its marginal efficiency) is higher (lower) than the monetary interest rate, the demand of such capital will increase (decrease): this is a choice assets mechanism.

Contrary to Piketty's hypothesis, the rate of interest is a key variable to explain, at the micro and macroeconomic level, the investment function: its level determines the last profitable investment (Pasinetti 1997, p. 215) and, consequently, the total capital.

1.2.3 The Value of an Aggregate Quantity of Capital

From a Neo-Ricardian/Cambridgean perspective, we can solve the problem related to the measurement of a quantity of aggregate capital and of the comparison of its evolution in different periods. As demonstrated by Ricardo and by the Neo-Ricardian school, such resolution implies in evaluating the dated labor in function of the current values of distributive variables.

We obtain the same kinds of results from the Ricardian theory of differential rent: the economic growth translates in an increase of the wheat demand, and as the wheat value is determined by the quantity of labor on the worst land, the wheat value increases at each period. *The Ricardian argument argues that the commodities value is determined by the economic growth and/or by a modification of the distributive variables*. This is a historical approach: the change in one of the exogenous variable (economic growth and/or distribution variables) implies a change in goods and capital value. *Inversely, the constant value of capital implies that distribution variables are constant during the period studied and that there is not economic growth.*

Piketty ignores such mechanism: he evaluates the stock of capital from the market prices and affirms that dynamic of the ratio capital/product may be analyzed independently of capital distribution (Piketty 2013, p. 268).[5] It is the reason why he interprets Harrod's hypothesis of constant coefficient of capital from the specificities of the technology (idem., pp. 165 and 166), and reduces Harrod's model to a short-run business cycle model (the "razor edge" interpretation).

Such affirmations show profound misunderstanding of the theoretical debate for the following reasons:

i. Harrod was aware of the Cambridge controversy. The hypothesis of a constant coefficient of capital is justified by such approach, and not by a technological constraint. As Solow demonstrated nearly twenty years after Harrod, the convergence toward the equilibrium position is realized when the substitution of the production factors is total. Reswitching of techniques demonstrates that such substitution mechanism is not valid for all values of the interest rate and, consequently, that substitution of production factors is limited. It is the reason why, in his model, Solow considers a single-good economy (1956).
ii. Piketty evaluates the capital in quantities. Then, he deduces the income distribution from these quantities; the way he interprets all the data is obligatory biased. It is not use to invoke the classical and Keynesian economists, as he does, using a neoclassical methodology, to formulate "heterodox" results. On the other hand, the intensification of inequalities in income distribution is verified when the substitution elasticity is higher than one. From a neoclassical perspective, this is an atypical production function.

[5]The French version (2013) is different from the English one (2014); I will use both.

2 The Main Methodological Oppositions

2.1 The Historical Approach

Polanyi affirms that the creation of wealth, in other mode of production that the capitalist one, "(...) does not depend on markets" (1983, p. 71). In Piketty's historical analysis, History is absent. If capital is the product of specific social relations, the measurement of its evolutions can be made only for the same historical period regulated by the same kind of social relations. The universalization of the concept of capital implies the permanency of this kind of social relations; as seen, such hypothesis must be refuted.

From an historical and anthropological perspective, we can affirm that the social forms of wealth have no relationship with the exchange value: for example, self-consumption, in regard to the anthropological concept of extended family, social use value or gift economy, in the sense defined by Mauss (1923–1924).

2.2 The Cambridgean Models

2.2.1 Kaldor's Model

The main results of Kaldor's model (1955–1956) are the following ones:

$$\frac{P}{Y} = \frac{1}{\text{sp} - \text{sw}} \cdot \frac{I}{Y} - \frac{\text{sw}}{\text{sp} - \text{sw}} \qquad (6)$$

(P is the profit, Y is the National Income, sp and sw are the capitalists and the worker's marginal propensity to save, and I is investment; sp > sw)

Such equation highlights the primacy of capitalists' expenditures: the profit share in the national income depends on capitalists' productive expenditures, i.e., on the investment (Idem., p. 96). If sp is low (because, for example, capitalists' consumption is high), the coefficient 1/sp−sw is high as the multiplier effect on the profit share; if *sw* is nil, we can observe a negative correlation between the marginal propensity to save of the capitalists and this multiplier effect.

Investment is an exogenous, i.e., an independent variable that does not depend on the marginal propensities to save (ibid., p. 95).

Then, we can write:

$$\frac{P}{K} = \frac{P}{Y} \cdot \frac{1}{v} \tag{7}$$

(v is the capital coefficient).

This mechanism shows that there is a negative correlation between the profit rate and the capital coefficient.

Harrod's model may be expressed in the following way:

$$I/Y = G \cdot v \tag{8}$$

(G is the income growth rate).

From (7) and (8)

$$\frac{P}{Y} = \frac{1}{\mathrm{sp} - \mathrm{sw}} \cdot G \cdot v - \frac{\mathrm{sw}}{\mathrm{sp} - \mathrm{sw}} \tag{9}$$

The logical problem is linked to the modalities of determination of the value of v, and once again to the relationship between the distributive variables (here the profit rate) and the value of v and Y: As writes Kaldor, "(…) G.v will be dependent on the rate of profit.(….) the value of particular capital goods in terms of final consumption goods will vary with the rate of profit" (1955–1956, p. 98) (Table 1).

In Kaldor's relations, the profit rate is endogenous and depends, in a negative way, on the coefficient of capital. This can be justified by the classical and Keynesian concept of abundance of capital. In Piketty's formulation, on the contrary, the profit rate is exogenous; this character exogenous is justified by some statistical regularities.

Table 1 Kaldor versus Piketty

Piketty	Kaldor
$\alpha = r.\beta$	$r = \alpha/\beta$
$\alpha = r.s/g$	$\alpha = g.\beta/s$

According to Piketty's framework, the profit relative share is positively determined by the profit rate and the rate of saving, and negatively by the rate of increase of the income. *We can note the crucial role of saving; this is a characteristic of neoclassical macroeconomic causality, i.e., Say's law*. The Kaldor's mechanisms are totally different: the profit relative share depends positively on the income rate of growth and on the coefficient of capital, and negatively on the rate of saving; such results are Keynesian (and Kaleckian): they highlight the positive role of expenditures on the profit share and the negative one of the rate of saving.

2.2.2 Pasinetti's Model

Pasinetti's model implies modifying the problematic linked to income distribution, from the distinction between profits and wages and capitalists and workers incomes (1962, p. 270): if workers save, they earn part of the global profit. The effective distribution of income is not limited to the distribution between wages and profits. There are two modalities of income distribution: the *functional* one concerns the distribution between wages and profits, and is directly connected with the production factors. The second one may be called *patrimonial distribution*: the income depends on the capital goods that were purchased from saving.

The main results may be expressed by the following equations:

$$\mathrm{Sw} = \mathrm{sw}(W + \mathrm{Pw}) \tag{10}$$

$$\mathrm{Sc} = \mathrm{sc} \cdot \mathrm{Pc} \tag{11}$$

Sw and Sc are workers' and capitalists' saving, Pw and Pc as workers' and capitalists' profit, *W* is wages, and sw and sp are workers and capitalists' marginal propensity to save. These equations express the mechanism linked to patrimonial distribution of income: workers and capitalists' saving depends on their respective incomes. In the long-run equilibrium position, we have:

$$\mathrm{Pw/Sw} = \mathrm{Pc/Sc} \tag{12}$$

The ratio of the profits to the saving is the same for workers and capitalists (idem., p. 272).

From (11) and (12), it is possible to deduce that:

$$Pc/Sc = 1/s_c = Pw/Sw \tag{13}$$

So, the workers' profit depends only on the capitalists' propensity to save. Such results are expressed in the following equations:

$$\frac{P}{K} = \frac{1}{s_c} \cdot \frac{I}{K} \tag{14}$$

$$\frac{\mathrm{P}}{\mathrm{Y}} = \frac{1}{\mathrm{sc}} \cdot \frac{\mathrm{I}}{\mathrm{Y}} \tag{15}$$

The total profit rate and the total profit share depend on the capitalists' productive expenditures; such ratios are determined independently from the workers' propensity to save. The total profit rate and the total profit share are entirely determined by the capitalists' decisions (ibid., pp. 273 and 274).

There is no reason to deduce that, systematically, income concentration will intensify; theoretically, the return on the patrimonial capital will be the same for the two social groups, as shown in Eq. (13). An intensification of the income concentration at the expense of workers only may be explained by a decrease of the wages in regard to profits.

On the other hand, Pasinetti's conception of capital is based on productive capital: the profit comes from the total profit generated by productive capital, in the productive sector: such conception is incompatible with Piketty's.

Final Remarks

In conclusion, we can affirm that Piketty's results are not based on a coherent and a trustworthy methodological framework. They come to an epistemological patchwork[6] without internal coherence. The

[6]Patchwork, in the sense Piketty uses various incompatible theoretical frameworks, and he does not respect the internal coherency of each one. Such observation may be applied both to the way Piketty uses orthodox and to heterodox frameworks.

abundance of data does not compensate the epistemological poverty and the methodological incoherence.

Moreover, one of the countless paradoxes present in this book may be expressed in these terms: Piketty wants to draw a long-term and exhaustive historical panorama of the income distribution without considering the changes in social and economic relations: he postulates the invariance of such relations, i.e., the absence of historicity.

If capital is defined as "the sum total of nonhuman assets that can be owned and exchanged on some market" (Piketty 2014, p. 38), the only condition that allows to study the evolution of capital from ancient times to 2100 AD (idem., p. 75) consists in postulating the existence of market as regulatory variables during all this period; this means denying the historical specificities of each period.

As Coase wrote (1994), if you torture the data long enough, it will confess; processing empirical data without defining beforehand a coherent framework is a manner to torture them; and they confessed what Mr. Piketty wanted them to confess.

References

Besomi, Daniele. 2001. Harrod's Dynamics and the Theory of Growth: The Story of a Mistaken Attribution. *Cambridge Journal of Economics* 25: 79–96.

Braudel, Fernand. 1979. *Civilisation matérielle, économie et capitalisme XVe-XVIIIème siècle. 2. Les jeux de l'échange*. Paris: Armand Colin.

———. 1985. *La dynamique du capitalisme*. Paris: Champs Flammarion.

Chick, Victoria. 1991. *Macroeconomics After Keynes: A Reconsideration of the General Theory*. Cambridge: First MIT Press Edition.

Coase, R.H. 1994. *Essays on Economics and Economists*. Chicago: University of Chicago Press.

Dávila-Fernández, Marwiland, and José Oreiro. 2016. Piketty in the Light of Pasinetti and Foley: Income Distribution, Economic Growth and Financial Fragility, *Revista de Economia Política* 36: 667–683, São Paolo.

Dumont, Louis. 1985. *Homo aequalis. Genèse et épanouissement de l'idéologie économique*. Paris: NRF, Editions Gallimard.

Felipe, Jesus, and J.S.L. McCombie. 2005. How Sound Are the Foundations of the Aggregate Production Function? *Eastern Economic Journal* 31 (3) (Summer): 467–488.

Harrod, Roy F. 1939. An Essay in Dynamic Theory. *The Economic Journal* 49: 14–33.

Herscovici, Alain. 2006a. O modelo de Harrod: natureza das expectativas de longo prazo, instabilidade e não-linearidade. *Economia e Sociedade, Campinas*, v. 15, n. 1 (26), p., jan./abr.

———. 2006b. Keynes e a teoria dos fundos de emprestimos:os fundamentos da critica de Keynes a economia (neo) clássica (Keynes and the loanable funds theory: the foundations of neoclassical economy critic), Análise Econômica, Ano 24, n. 46, setembro 2006, Faculdade de Ciências Econômicas, UFRGS, Porto Alegre.

Kaldor, Nicholas. 1955–1956. Alternative Theories of Distribution. *The Review of Economic Studies* 23 (2): 83–100.

Keynes, John Maynard. 2009. *The General Theory of Employment, Interest and Money*. New York: Classic Books America.

Kregel, J. 1980. Markets and institutions as features of a capitalistic production system. *Journal of Post-keynesian Economics/Fall* III (1): 32–49.

Lakatos, Imre. 1978. *The Methodology of Scientific Research Programs*. Philosophical Papers Volume I. Edited by John Worral and Gregory Currie. Cambridge: Cambridge University Press.

Mauss, Marcel. 1923–1924. Essai sur le don. *l'année sociologique* 1: 30–186.

Orléan, André. 2011. *L'empire de la valeur. Refonder l'Économie*. Paris: Éditions du Seuil.

Pasinetti, Luigi L. 1962. Rate of Profit and Income Distribution in Relation to the Rate of Economic Growth. *The Review of Economic Studies* 29 (4) (October): 267–279.

———. 1997. The Marginal Efficiency of Investment. In *A "Second Edition" of the General Theory-Vol. 1*, ed. G.C. Harcourt and P.A. Riach, 198–218. London: Routledge.

Polanyi, Karl. 1983. *La Grande Transformation. Aux origines politiques et économiques de notre temps*. Paris: Editions Gallimard.

Ricardo, David. 1821. *On the Principles of Political Economy and Taxation*, 3rd ed. Ontario: Batoche Book 2001.

Thomas, Piketty. 2014. *Capital in the Twenty First Century*. Cambridge, MA and London: The Belknap Press of Harvard University Press.

———. 2013. *Le capital au XXIème siècle*. Paris: Editions du Seuil.

Solow, R. 1956. A Contribution to the Theory of Economic Growth. *Quarterly Journal of Economics* 70: 65–94.

———. 2014. Everything You Need to Know About 'Capital in the Twenty-First Century'. http://www.newrepublic.com/article/117429/capital-twenty-first-century-thomaspikettyreviewed. Accessed 14 December 2015.

Vercelli, Alessandro. 1991. *Methodological Foundations of Macroeconomics: Keynes and Lucas*. Cambridge: Cambridge University Press.

9
General Conclusion

In conclusion, we can affirm, without ambiguity, that capital historicity is a criterion that allows delimiting the epistemological rupture between the different Schools: the very object of Economics, the kind of micro and macro causalities and the way empirical instruments are designed to study the empirical data will be different.

The substantial hypothesis was adopted by the Physiocrats, by Adam Smith and by all the neoclassical school: Capital is conceived as a natural process inherent to "human nature". Capital is evaluated from its quantities; such quantities have the same value in all the periods considered. This "naturalism" is present in all the neoclassical construction: rationality, for example, is purely supra-historical, and allows explaining the agents' behavior regardless of any historical and sociological determinism (Godelier 1969). This choice implies in elaborating a universal theory, in the Popperian sense.

On the other hand, the Ricardian and the Keynesian schools refute such universalism: they aim at elaborating a historical analysis and its explanation is obligatorily limited to some specific initial conditions, i.e., to some historical period. If such approach is more limited, it is more realistic.

A. Herscovici, *Essays on the Historicity of Capital*,
https://doi.org/10.1007/978-3-030-14838-6_9

Contrary to the common affirmation, Ricardo's method is not purely "hypothetical and deductive" (Blaug 1992), in the sense that capital value depends directly on historical variables related to rent distribution. From the same perspective, Keynes's method is similar, as capital value depends on long-term expectations, and as such expectation move upon time. Finally, from Akerlof, Grossman and Stiglitz's works, we can say that Economy is essentially "relational": value production is an endogenous mechanism explained from the interrelations between agents. So, capital is obligatorily heterogeneous, and its value changes over time.

The neoclassical school allows maintaining its universal dimension from some logical hypotheses that are particularly questionable, from an economic perspective: if we consider Ricardo's and Keynes' update mechanisms, the marginalist calculus constitutes an inappropriate tool to be applied in Economic amounts (Marcuzzo and Rosselli 2011; Dvoskin and Fratini 2016): the marginal modifications cannot be limited to the marginal magnitudes, but they will apply to the whole magnitude. Contrary to the common idea, neoclassical, and not Ricardian economics, is essentially hypothetical-deductive, and such *démarche* is inappropriate in Economics.

On the contrary, the Ricardian, Keynesian and Stiglitzian economics focuses on the capital heterogeneity, which translates into an historical approach: such epistemological choice allows using a historical time and explaining short- and long-run changes and its relationships.

In the last instance, we can affirm that the debate between universalism and historicism is directly related to the debate determinism versus indeterminism. While the former concerns the convergence toward a stable equilibrium, the latter is related to the structural instability (Vercelli 1985, 1991), and to the methodological indeterminism (Herscovici 2002). Such choice characterizes the modern epistemology, in regard to all scientific fields, and favors the study of complex system from its historical dimension.

References

Blaug, Mark. 1992. *The Methodology of Economics or How Economists Explain*, 2nd ed. Cambridge: Cambridge University Press.

Dvoskin, Ariel, and Saverio M. Fratini. 2016. On the Samuelson-Etula Master Function and the Capital Controversy. *The European Journal of the History of Economic Thought* 23 (6): 1032–1058.

Godelier, Maurice. 1969. *Rationalité et irrationalité en économie*. Paris: Librairie François Maspéro.

Herscovici, Alain. 2002. *Dinâmica Macroeconômica: uma interpretação a partir de Marx e de Keynes*. São Paulo: EDUC/EDUFES.

Marcuzzo, Maria Cristina, and Rosselli Annalisa. 2011. Sraffa and His Arguments Against 'Marginism'. *Cambridge Journal of Economics* 35: 219–231.

Vercelli, Alessandro. 1985. Keynes, Schumpeter, Marx and the Structural Instability of Capitalism. In *L'hétérodoxie dans la pensée économique*, org. G. Deleplace and P. Maurisson. Paris: Cahiers d'Economie Politique, Anthropos.

———. 1991. *Methodological Foundations of Macroeconomics: Keynes and Lucas*. Cambridge: Cambridge University Press.

Printed by Printforce, the Netherlands